Economics and Sociology: Towards an Integration

Economics and Sociology:
Towards an Integration

Edited by
T. Huppes
University of Groningen

Springer-Science+Business Media, B.V.

Library of Congress Cataloging in Publication Data

Main entry under title:

Economics and sociology.

Reprint. Originally published: Leiden:
M. Nijhoff Social Sciences Division, 1976.
Includes bibliographical references.
1. Economics-Addresses, essays, lectures.
2. Sociology-Addresses, essays, lectures.
I. Huppes, T.
HM35.E25 1982 306'.3 81-20806
AACR2

ISBN 978-94-017-1370-2 ISBN 978-94-017-1368-9 (eBook)
DOI 10.1007/978-94-017-1368-9

Originally published by H.E. Stenfert Kroese B.V., Leiden in 1976.
Softcover reprint of the hardcover 1st edition 1976
Second printing 1982

Preface

In recent years economics has been the subject of increasingly severe criticism. It has failed both to predict and to counteract the economic crisis now afflicting nearly the whole Western world. Economic life is more disrupted than ever:

- the rate of inflation has risen alarmingly
- unemployment has not been as high since the 1930s
- economic growth is stagnating
- there is increasing opposition to the inequality in the distribution of income and wealth, on a national scale as well as in the world at large
- the process of economic integration (EEC, GATT, UNCTAD) is being thwarted
- programmes of economic development in the third world have not produced the desired effects
- etcetera.

Obviously, it would not be fair to put the blame for the crisis on economic science. But the present predicament does call for serious consideration of the limitations of economic explanation. Among the social sciences, economics is unquestionably the most advanced discipline. Its very sophistication, however, leads it to abstract from social phenomena such as norms, institutions, power, conflict and social change. Thus the manifest influence of sociological variables on the course of economic processes remains hidden.

Dominating this book as a drumbeat is the conviction held by the several authors that a clearer grasp of the current problems may be obtained if economists and sociologists are prepared to co-operate more closely. An interdisciplinary approach is warranted; the distinction between the social sciences should be less sharply drawn.

The separate chapters of this book were first written as discussion papers for the Symposium *Economics and Sociology: Towards an Integration,* organised by the Department of Economics, Groningen

University, in September 1975. Among the participants were economists and sociologists from nearly all the Dutch universities. For two days the village of Gieten (Dr.) was the scene of a unique confrontation between economics and sociology, during which the integration of the two disciplines was approached from various angles. The concluding chapter of this book by Adam Szirmai, Groningen, gives an impression of this event.

Contributions towards the integration of economics and sociology are found in both disciplines, particularly in economic sociology and institutional economics. Both are represented twice in this book. In addition a paper has been included on the problem of integration approached from the methodological viewpoint. Finally, an example of 'applied integration' is presented in the form of an interdisciplinary analysis of a concrete economic problem: inflation.

Economic sociology studies economic processes from a sociological frame of reference. In chapter 1 the functionalist viewpoint is represented by Neil J. Smelser from Berkeley, California. 'The relevance of economic sociology for economics' is illustrated by way of two examples: the sociological analysis of economic rationality, and an analysis of the social implications of economic stagnation.

In my own contribution in chapter 2, I approach the integration economics-sociology from the angle of social exchange theory. This school of thought works with a paradigm similar to that of neoclassical economics. George C. Homans, the first to bring the concept of social exchange into prominence, is taken as a point of departure. After confronting his theory with the neoclassical equilibrium model, an effort is made to develop an interdisciplinary conception of society.

Unlike economic sociology, which is generally acknowledged as an independent specialism, institutional economics is hardly accepted as such in Holland. Originating in the U.S. at the beginning of this century as a reaction to neoclassical economics, it has been popular in that country ever since. The founder of institutionalism is the economist and sociologist Thorstein Veblen. Today this school of thought is represented by John K. Galbraith, Robert L. Heilbroner, Gunnar Myrdal, Allan G. Gruchy, K. William Kapp and others. Institutionalists may be distinguished from the neoclassical mainstream by the special attention they give to sociological variables. In Gruchy's words: they study 'the changing pattern of cultural relations which deal with the creation and disposal of scarce material goods and services by individuals and groups in the light of their private and public aims'. In various publications Gruchy has applied himself to the difficult task of ordering the frequently diverging contributions of the institutionalists. In chapter 3 he discusses the importance of institutional economics for an interdisciplinary approach of social and economic problems.

In April 1976, while still at work on the manuscript of his book, I received the sad news of professor K. William Kapp's unexpected death. Kapp was one of Europe's best known institutionalists. His views were close to Myrdal's as will appear from his contribution to the Symposium in chapter 4.

As far as I know the integration of economics and sociology has never been approached from a methodological perspective. Only few scientists are familiar with the research methods of both disciplines. In chapter 5 Ivan Gadourek, Groningen, gives an account of his scrutiny of 'the convergence and diversification in methodologies of economics and sociology'. His paper shows how both sociologists and economists might learn from each other's methods and techniques of research.

As an example of 'applied integration' the connection between the level of inflation and the degree of anomie in a society is examined in chapter 6. Inflation is normally considered to be a subject within the domain of economics; anomie is a phenomenon studied by sociologists. The idea that the two phenomena are related is based on the interdisciplinary conception as developed in chapter 2.

The integration of economics and sociology is no easy matter. The various chapters of this book should not be regarded as definite solutions to the problem. They provide possible lines of access. I should add, moreover, that this book contains only a selection of the various ways in which the problem of integration may be dealt with. Neo-marxism and general systems theory, for instance, are not represented. The main purpose is not to present a complete picture but to stimulate the interest in the integration of the two disciplines. I hope the book will serve this purpose.

T.H.

University of Groningen
June, 1976.

Contents

List of contributors

Ivan Gadourek, Professor of Sociology, University of Groningen.

Allan G. Gruchy, Professor of Economics, University of Maryland, U.S.A.

Tjerk Huppes, Assistant professor of Economics and Sociology, University of Groningen.

K. William Kapp †, Professor of Economics, University of Basel, Switzerland.

Neil J. Smelser, Professor of Sociology, Berkeley, University of California, U.S.A.

Adam Szirmai, Assistant Professor of Sociology, University of Groningen.

1. On the relevance of economic sociology for economics

Neil J. Smelser

1.1. Introduction and definition of terms

So many and so complex are the linkages between the economy and its socio-cultural environment that it is almost impossible to summarize the relevance of economic sociology for economics in the compass of a short paper. Accordingly, in what follows I am forced to be both somewhat cryptic and somewhat selective in my emphases.

I begin with a few preliminary definitions of terms. With Samuelson, I define economics as

> '... the study of how men and society end up *choosing*, with or without the use of money, to employ scarce productive resources that could have alternative uses, to produce various commodities and distribute them for consumption, now or in the future, among various people and groups in society'.[1]

I define sociology as the systematic effort to explain regularities and variations in individual orientations and behavior, group orientations and behavior, social structures, sanctions, norms, and values; more specifically, sociology studies the causal and interactive processes that relate these several types of variables to one another.[2]

Finally, I define economic sociology as the application of the frames of reference, variables, and explanatory models of sociology to that complex of activities concerned with the production, distribution, exchange and consumption of scarce goods and services.

1. Paul A. Samuelson, *Economics,* 9th ed. (New York: McGraw-Hill, 1973), p. 3. A more concise, but essentially similar definition is given by Bronfenbrenner: 'Economics is the systematic study of social adjustment to, and management of, the scarcity of goods and resources'. Martin Bronfenbrenner, 'A "Middlebrow" Introduction to Economic Methodology', in Sherman Roy Krupp (ed.), *The Structure of Economic Science: Essays on Methodology* (Englewood Cliffs, New Jersey: Prentice-Hall, 1966), p. 6.
2. A more elaborated definition may be found in Neil J. Smelser, (ed.), *Sociology: An Introduction,* second edition, (New York: Wiley, 1973).

This definition suggests that the economic sociologist asks two types of questions. The first is microscopic, and concerns *economic activities* as such. The economic sociologist asks how these activities are structured into roles and collectivities, by what values they are legitimized, and by what norms and sanctions they are regulated. And within economic organizations, such as the firm, he studies the status system, power and authority relations, deviance, and cliques and coalitions as these affect the economic activities of the firm.

The second type of question is macroscopic, and concerns the relations between sociological variables as they manifest themselves in *economic* contexts and sociological variables as they manifest themselves in *non-economic* contexts. For example, what sorts of political conflict are generated by the economic arrangements in different societies? What kinds of class systems emerge in different kinds of economic systems?

In the opening section of the paper I shall approach the microscopic type of question by examining certain assumptions made by economists regarding non-economic variables – assumptions associated in particular with the issue of *economic rationality* – and indicating how economic sociology can help correct, refine, and elaborate such assumptions. In the next section of the paper I shall approach the macroscopic type of question by asking, what sorts of non-economic processes may be expected to appear under conditions of long-term stagnation or decline of economic activity. In a final section of the paper I shall venture a few speculations on the relevance of economic sociology to economic policy decisions.

1.2. The status of economic rationality as a parameter of economic activity

Versions of *economic rationality*. One of the most important postulates in traditional economic analysis is some version of economic rationality: If an individual is presented with a situation of choice in an economic setting, he will maximize or optimize his economic position; likewise, a firm will 'choose the [input-output combination] which maximizes the difference between its total costs and revenues'.[3] Such a postulate may

3. Wassily Leontief, 'Mathematics in Economics', in *Essays in Economics: Theories and*

be informed by different varieties of utility functions, but despite this variability, it retains its character as a statement of *criteria for choice in scarcity situations,* and constitutes one of the fundamental building blocks for predicting economic behavior, both for the individual and in the aggregate.

Several versions of this postulate have been criticized and more or less discredited – namely the version that material satisfactions are the sole motivating factor in human existence, and that people actually behave rationally when faced with economic decisions.[4] Most economists treat the notion of economic rationality as a matter of analytic convenience; they do not advance it as a psychological theory, but rather as a way of simplifying the enormous motivational variability of the empirical world, and proceed *as if* the only independent variables are measurable changes in price and income. Regarded as such, the notion is a valuable device, for it permits the economist to reduce the number of potentially operative variables to a manageable number and to construct concise models of economic behavior.

In contrast to these several versions of the postulate of economic rationality, the economic sociologist tends to consider it as an institutionalized value.[5] In this version rationality becomes something more than a psychological postulate; it is a standard of behavior to which people conform or from which they deviate. Thus in a business firm in a capitalist society it is not only the businessman's personal desire for profits but also the threat of negative social sanctions (for example, ridicule or loss of position) that encourages him to follow the criteria of efficiency and cost-reduction. Viewed in this way, economic rationality becomes a type of social control – exercised through the internalization of materialistic values and values of 'efficiency'; through the institutionalization of systems of positive and negative sanctions. It becomes a typical motivational and attitudinal complex that is acquired through socialization and sustained by institutional arrangements. Furthermore, when viewed in this way, the notion of economic rationality becomes an empirical variable rather than a fixed postulate, from the *methodological*

Theorizing (New York: Oxford University Press, 1966), p. 23. For a recent discussion of utility functions and 'economic man', see Jerome Rothenberg, 'Values and Value Theory in Economics', in Krupp (ed.), *The Structure of Economic Science, op. cit.,* p. 6.

4. Unless, in fact, the utility function is characterized in such general and indeterminate terms that every act can be characterized as rational by definition.

5. Talcott Parsons and Neil J. Smelser, *Economy and Society* (Glencoe, Ill.: The Free Press, 1956), p. 175.

point of view. And finally, the notion of economic rationality emerges as a number of simplified, *substantive* assumptions concerning the operation of typical sociological variables of values, norms, and sanctions.

1.2.1. Research developments relating to how non-economic 'rationalities' shape economic activity

A number of recent research developments have pointed to conditions under which the substantive assumptions of the postulate of economic rationality do not hold empirically – that is to say, conditions under which principles of rational economic calculation are minimized or subordinated to some other kind of 'rationality' and under which the sanctions for controlling the movement of economic goods and services are non-economic sanctions. Among these developments are the following:

1. One line of interest in comparative exchange was stirred by the appearance in the late 1950's of a volume edited by Polanyi, Arensberg, and Pearson.[6] Roaming through the records of Babylon, Mesopotamia, Greece, Mexico, Yucatan and village India, they sketched a picture of the separation of trading practices from the familiar practices of free-market exchange. In addition, they prepared a critique of the analytic power of traditional economic theory and suggested some alternatives for a better comparative economics.

Polanyi and his associates suggested that economic activities fall into three main patterns of exchange. The first, which they call *reciprocative,* is illustrated by the ritualized gift-giving among families, clans and tribes. Another illustration is found among farmers of many civilizations, who frequently pitch in to work for one another, especially at harvest times. Economic calculation, price payments, and wages are typically absent in these types of exchange. Goods or services are given because it is traditional to do so; the only principle of calculation is the loose principle that the giving and receiving of goods or services should balance out among the exchanging parties in the long run.

The second pattern of exchange is *redistributive.* This brings economic goods and services to a central source – usually governmental – and then

6. Karl Polanyi, Conrad Arensberg and Harry Pearson, *Trade and Market in the Early Empires* (Glencoe, Ill.: The Free Press and the Falcon's Wing Press, 1957).

redistributes them throughout the populace. Polanyi, Arensberg and Pearson identified several instances of this exchange pattern in ancient Asian and African civilizations. Modern examples are organized charity and progressive taxation. Like reciprocative exchange, redistributive patterns are often characterized by an absence of economic calculation. In this case the principle of calculation seems to be one of justice or equity – that is, what each class of recipients deserves by some standard.

The third pattern of exchange, more familiar in modern Western civilization, was termed, simply, *exchange*. In this case economic goods and services are brought into a market context. Prices are not standardized on the basis of tradition, but result from bargaining for economic advantage.

Sahlins extended and elaborated the model of reciprocative exchange by distinguishing among several types of reciprocity. The first is 'generalized' reciprocity, which is putatively altruistic and for which any obligation for repayment is suppressed or left indefinite. The clearest example is food-sharing with members of a nuclear family. At most, receiving the food (say, by young children) 'lays on a diffuse obligation to reciprocate when necessary to the donor and/or possibly for the recipient'.[7] The second is 'balanced' reciprocity, in which there is an expectation of repayment of an equivalent without delay, in the case of marital settlements or peace agreements. This form is more calculated, less personal than the first. The third is 'negative' reciprocity, or 'the attempt to get something for nothing with impunity, as in haggling, gambling, stealing, or plundering'. Sahlins went on to argue that the best way to predict which type of reciprocity will dominate is to trace the 'kinship distance' between parties; and he pulled together ethnographic data on patterns of giving and taking to demonstrate his central hypothesis that '[reciprocity] is inclined toward the generalized pole by close kinship, toward the negative extreme in proportion to kinship distance'.[8]

In a markedly different kind of analysis, Titmuss investigated international differences in patterns of blood donation. This unusual form of gift – which is in one sense an act of generalized reciprocity in that nothing is expected in return, and in another sense an anonymous, impersonal act – has survived in large part as a voluntary, unrewarded

7. Marshall Sahlins, 'On the Sociology of Primitive Exchange', in *Stone Age Economics* (Chicago: Aldine-Atherton, 1972), p. 186.
8. *Ibid.*, p. 196.

act in a few societies, such as Great Britain, but in other societies blood has become, in part, a marketable and even a profitable commodity. In the United States and the Soviet Union, for example, fully half the blood donors are paid, and in Japan almost all donors receive money for giving blood. Titmuss was far from being able to account for such international differences, but he speculated that the best place to look is in the 'fabric of values, social, economic, and political, within which acts of giving, rewarding, compelling or selling take place'.[9]

2. Another line of interest in nonmarket transfers has been stimulated by scholars working on communist and socialist societies. These kinds of societies, characterized in ideal-typical terms, have a central authority that owns all the means of production, determines consumption through physical rationing, and assigns labor at predetermined wages. Thus characterized, the 'command economy' leaves little room for market exchange.[10] In practice, of course, communist and socialist economies have not even approximated the ideal type, and many market mechanisms have developed alongside the dominant political mechanism, just as many market economies have supplemented their major economic mechanism by a greater reliance on political and administrative controls.[11] However, while acknowledging that any given economy relies on a number of different mechanisms, Grossman nevertheless felt it appropriate to classify economies in terms of which kind of mechanism is *dominant*: tradition, or 'generally accepted, customary, and persistent specific patterns of relationship among economic units or agents'; market; and command.[12] This classification is not completely unlike that of Polanyi, Arensberg, and Pearson, though their notion of 'redistributive exchange' also contains many traditional elements. In terms of sanctions, the market economy relies mainly on economic sanctions, the command economy mainly on political sanctions, and the traditional economy on a residual group of social and political sanctions. In a quite different spirit, Galbraith, in his presidential address to the American

9. Richard Titmuss, *The Gift Relationship: From Human Blood to Social Policy* (London: George Allen and Unwin, 1970), p. 179.

10. See Oleg Zinam, 'The Economics of Command Economies', in Jan S. Prybyla (ed.), *Comparative Economic Systems* (New York: Appleton-Century-Crofts, 1969), p. 16.

11. For an introductory characterization of the 'mixed' character of the Soviet economy, see William N. Loucks and William G. Whitney, *Comparative Economic Systems*, eighth edition (New York: Harper and Row, 1969), pp. 392-532.

12. Gregory Grossman, *Economic Systems*, second edition (Englewood Cliffs, New Jersey: Prentice-Hall, 1974), pp. 18-20.

Economic Association, complained that neo-classical and neo-Keynesian economic frameworks are incapable of analyzing the concentration of planning and power in the modern American economy, primarily because they have focussed too much on market processes and have made economics a 'non-political subject'.[13] While not implying that America is a command economy, Galbraith was nonetheless asserting that a significant amount of its economic activity transpires under the umbrella of some sort of 'political rationality' for which traditional assumptions about economic rationality and the market are not appropriate.

3. Still another line of interest in nonmarket transfers is found in the growing interest in the grants economy. By 'grants' is meant a 'one-way economic relationship whereby party A conveys an exchangeable to party B without receiving in turn an exchangeable of equal market value'.[14] This contrasts with the two-way exchange characteristic of market transactions, in which both parties receive economic consideration. Examples of grants are redistribution through taxation, charity donations, foundation grants, public support of children, as well as intrafamilial transfers of goods and services. The grant is defined in economic terms, and while Boulding acknowledged that a transfer from A to B 'may be accompanied by certain intangible transfers from B to A in the way of prestige, status, and so on', he added that 'these things are not usually classified as exchangeables'.[15] This exclusion is unfortunate in a way, since so many economic grants are locked into a system of other kinds of rewards for the grantor – the politician who distributes benefits to the poor in return for votes and power, the philanthropist who secures prestige in the public eye for his good works, and the like. Despite this restriction, Boulding regarded grants as having primary significance not in the economic system but rather in the 'integrative structure of society'; furthermore, they are reflective of relationships of community, legitimacy, loyalty, love and trust.[16] He suggested further that the great increase in public grants in recent decades might be

13. John K. Galbraith, 'Power and the Useful Economist', *American Economic Review*, Vol. 63 (1973), pp. 1-12.
14. Kenneth E. Boulding, 'Urbanization and the Grants Economy: An Introduction', in Kenneth E. Boulding, Martin Pfaff and Anita Pfaff (eds.), *Transfers in an Urbanized Economy* (Belmont California: Wadsworth Publishing Co., 1973), p. 1.
15. Kenneth E. Boulding, 'The Grants Economy', in *Collected Papers*, edited by Fred R. Glahe (Boulder, Colorado: University of Colorado Press, 1971) p. 477.
16. *Ibid.*, p. 478.

regarded as an 'integrative' compensation for the decline of private transfers in financing health, education and welfare, and for the relative decline of the extended family – a private, 'granting' agency *par excellence.*[17] Whatever the merits of this particular theoretical formulation, the focus on one-way exchanges has led economists to begin asking new kinds of questions about exchange in society, such as whether suburban communities compensate central cities for the services they provide, whether transfer payments through welfare have a substantial impact on poverty in the ghettos, and the like.[18]

1.2.2. Relations among different 'rationalities'

The lines of research I have summarized suggest that in many cases the rationality of economic calculation is subordinated to other kinds of considerations. It is possible to press the inquiry even further, however, and ask if any *other* kinds of relations obtain among the different modes of structuring economic activity. Do different 'rationalities' come into *conflict* with one another, and, if so, what are the likely outcomes?

In addressing this question I shall refer to Max Weber's insights regarding the relations between economic rationality and what might be called 'communal rationality' – a phenomenon which has some elements of 'reciprocative' and 'redistributive' modes specified by Polanyi, *et al.*, and some elements of the 'integrative' mode which Boulding identified as a conspicuous feature of economic grants.

In his later methodological writings Weber gave great scientific importance to models based on assumptions about typical motives in typical situations. 'It is', he noted 'precisely on the basis of... rational assumptions [about meaning] that most of the laws of sociology, including those of economics, are built up'.[19] And the bulk of Weber's sociological work consists in the creation of historical models of varying levels of generality – for example, the model of bureaucracy, the model of charismatic leadership – and using these models as generalized interpretative frameworks to throw light on historical processes and developments. Weber was aware that to apply a single model to a

17. Boulding, 'Urbanization and the Grants Economy', *op. cit.*
18. *Ibid.*, Chapters 1-6.
19. Max Weber, *Economy and Society: An Outline of Interpretive Sociology*, edited by Guenter Roth and Claus Wittich (New York: Bedminster Press, 1968), Vol. I, p. 19.

historical situation constitutes an oversimplification, and that the proper strategy is to apply a battery of them successively to gain a firmer understanding of the diversity of historical causes operating in that situation.[20]

To create and use type models – among which would be models of economic rationality – carries knowledge to a certain level, but, to carry it further, models must be systematically compared among one another. This comparison involves a two-step process. First, the investigator must systematically explore the ways in which the implications of several models (that is, predicted courses of action) *reinforce* one another, are *independent* of one another, or call for *conflicting* courses of action. He must also specify – for example, in cases of conflicting courses of action – the conditions under which the forces of one historical model might prevail over the other, or what kinds of 'compromise' lines of action might emerge. What arises from this operation would be a new series of hypotheses (statements of anticipated lines of action) based on combinations of models. The second step, as in the case of a single historical model, is to assess the hypotheses in the light of the best historical data.

In his historical sociology Weber made numerous comparisons and contrasts among models. His famous discussion of types of authority, for example, is in part a discussion of the ways that charismatic, traditional, and rational-legal authority are oriented to issues such as how compliance with orders is secured, how financial support is maintained, and so on.[21] His comparisons, as a rule, were not as systematic as the procedures suggested in the preceding paragraph. Nevertheless, several of them are very suggestive. In particular his remarks on the relations between his ideal type model of economic rationality and communal rationality provide a basis for suggesting the strategy for investigating the relations among different rationalities on a systematic basis. Let me summarize and extend his reflections.

The themes that underscore the model of economic rationality developed by Weber are the *flexibility* of action that results from the autonomy of an enterprise, and the calculability of action on the basis of considerations of economic utility, free from the intrusion of non-economic considerations. Thus, Weber regarded the 'typical measures of

20. Guenter Roth, 'Max Weber's Comparative Approach and Historical Typology', in Ivan Vallier (ed.), *Comparative Methods in Sociology* (Berkeley: University of California Press, 1971), pp. 92-93.
21. *Economy and Society, op. cit.*, Vol. 1, pp. 212-254.

rational economic action' as the systematic allocation of utilities based on considerations of marginal utility, and the systematic procurement and control of the means of production.[22] Rationality of markets is based on market freedom and the reduction of the criteria of kinship, status privileges, military needs and community welfare in determining the distribution of resources and products.[23]

Weber did not develop a model of 'communal rationality' as explicit as that of economic rationality. Nevertheless, his writings on economic sociology are scattered with observations that suggest that this kind of orientation – of which the kinship unit provides the type illustration – contrasts on most counts with the model of economic rationality. Communal memberships rest on 'various types of affectual, emotional, or traditional bases', as in the case of a religious brotherhood or an erotic relationship.[24] Members in communal units have mutual responsibility for one another's welfare. Membership in many such units, including the family, is in large part compulsory in that, for example, an individual cannot freely choose his parents. The principle of distribution of resources is substantive rationality, or, broadly speaking, the principle of common welfare of members. This principle 'may consider the "purely formal" rationality of calculation in money terms as of quite secondary importance or even as fundamentally inimical to their respective ultimate ends'.[25]

In any empirical case, of course, an association based on calculation (for example, a market) does develop emotional (communal) aspects and an association based on communal values is not entirely free from considerations of expediency, calculation and exploitation.[26] Nevertheless, in principle, the criteria of calculation and the criteria of communality are opposed, and both cannot be maximized in the same situation.

As the values of economic rationality advanced and became consolidated in the West, therefore, communally-based associations could not remain indifferent to the institutionalization of these values. The main institutional mechanism that developed to mediate potential conflict between the two principles was that of segregation or differentiation. The

22. *Ibid.*, p. 71.
23. *Ibid.*, p. 83.
24. *Ibid.*, p. 41.
25. *Ibid.*, p. 86.
26. *Ibid.*, p. 107.

'sphere of private affairs' tended to become separated from the 'sphere of business affairs'.[27] Furthermore, this tendency was not 'fortuitous':

'It is a consequence of the fact that, from the point of view of business interest, the interest in maintaining the private wealth of the owner is often irrational, as is his interest in income receipts at any given time from the point of view of the profitability of the enterprise. Considerations relevant to the profitability of a business enterprise are also not identical with those governing the private interests of persons who are related to it as workers or as consumers. Conversely, the interests growing out of the private fortunes and income of persons or organizations having powers of control over an enterprise do not necessarily lie in the same direction as the long-run considerations of optimizing its profitability and its market power position. This is definitely, even especially true, when a profit-making enterprise is controlled by the producers' co-operative association. The objective interests of rational management of a business enterprise and the personal interests of the individuals who control it are by no means identical and are often opposed. This fact implies the separation as a matter of principle of the budgetary unit and the enterprise, even where both, with respect to powers of control and the objects controlled, are identical'.[28]

The separation is not entirely symmetrical, however; the family loses in the process. There is a 'weakening of household authority'. Because of the multiplication of life chances and opportunities, 'the individual becomes less and less content with being bound to rigid and undifferentiated forms of life prescribed by the group'.[29] Because the family also shrinks from the standpoint of size, resources, and functions:

'It is becoming increasingly inopportune for an individual to join a large communistic household. An individual no longer gets protection from the household and kinship groups, but rather from political authority, which exercises compulsory jurisdiction. Furthermore, household and occupation become ecologically separated, and the household is no longer a unit of common production but of common consumption. Moreover, the individual receives his entire education increasingly from outside his home and by means which are supplied by various enterprises: schools, bookstores, concert halls, clubs, meetings, etc. He can no longer regard the household as the bearer of those cultural values in whose service he places himself'.[30]

Weber was careful, however, not to press his argument concerning 'the parallelism of money economy and attenuation of household authority' to its ultimate. Domestic authority and household are 'relatively independent of economic conditions' and in fact 'they often shape economic relationships because of their own historic structure'.[31]

27. *Ibid.*, pp. 41-42.
28. *Ibid.*, p. 98.
29. *Ibid.*, p. 375.
30. *Ibid.*, p. 377.
31. *Ibid.*, p. 381.

In these passages Weber was, in effect, undertaking the task of comparing two ideal-type models – one of economic rationality and one of communal rationality – establishing a relation of opposition or conflict between them, and generating a number of 'predictions' of historical developments arising from these relations, especially predictions of compromise through structural separation and an accompanying defeat for communal rationality. He qualified his analysis, moreover, sufficiently to render ambiguous his ultimate judgment of the historical fate of communal rationality in the family in an environment of large-scale corporate enterprises and a money economy.

If one includes Weber's significant qualifications on his major thesis, there are in his analysis three distinguishable assertions concerning the relationship between an institutionalized system of economic rationality and the kinship structure:

- The family as an institutional system experiences a decline in significance;
- The family remains 'relatively independent of economic conditions';
- The family 'often shapes economic relationships'.

A variety of empirical illustrations for each of the three assertions could no doubt be produced. But one of the less satisfying aspects of Weber's analysis is that while envisioning these different possibilities, he did little by way of specifying the conditions under which each might be most likely to occur. As a result, his analysis of the relations between the institutionalization of economic rationality in the economy and the institutionalization of communal rationality in the family remains quite indeterminate.

1.2.3. A concluding note

All the various lines of research and argumentation on which I have touched – the work on reciprocation and redistribution, the work on command economies and grants economy, and Weber's reflections on economic and communal rationality – are so many different ways of discovering and pointing out that economic activity is embedded in a network of both economic and non-economic structures, rationalities, and sanctions.

One moral to be drawn from this fundamental fact of embeddedness is that any pure model of economic rationality – or any other kind of rationality, for that matter – is severely limited as a *general* basis for the understanding of economic activity. But I do not believe that this conclusion warrants abandoning such models. They have proved useful if not necessary devices for both theory-building and empirical investigation in economics and other social sciences. Rather, investigators should use such models in expanded and more complicated ways – along the following lines:

1. Systematic attention should be given to cataloguing the different kinds of 'rationalities' that can govern the production, distribution, and consumption of economic goods and services – the rationalities of efficiency, social justice, social security in the broad sense, military defense, and so on. Each kind of rationality has its own peculiar implications for directives and priorities for economic activities, for economic growth and stagnation, and for cumulative imbalances and injustices. Tracing out these implications means giving higher priority to constructing formal models of economic behavior on assumptions other than economic calculation.

2. Perhaps more important, systematic attention should be given to developing models that incorporate or synthesize a number of single models of rationality in different *combinations*. Most economically-relevant decisions – and the behavior that flows from them – that are made in contemporary times are not the product of a single type of calculation; they are complicated compromises that incorporate criteria arising from the exigencies of economic rationality, social justice, environmental protection, and others. It is possible to represent some of these criteria – for example, environmental protection – simply as 'costs' to be taken into account. Above and beyond that, however, they constitute fundamental forces in social life, and can be more systematically incorporated into more complex models of economic and social processes than we now have. In the longer run, too, it seems appropriate to construct models of the historical relations among different systems of rationality – such as Weber started to do – to help determine conditions under which different principles and criteria of organizing social and economic life complement one another, come into conflict, defeat one another, or are forged into 'compromise' institutional forms. If we regard the relations between economic and communal rationality as simply opposed to one another – as Weber tended to do – we shall observe research findings that are inconsistent and apparently contradictory. To improve such research it is necessary to do more than merely conduct

more research; it must be research that is based on more complicated models combining the economic and social rationalities that constitute the institutionalized motivational determinants of behavior.

1.3. Economic stagnation and its relation to the social order

Up to this point my remarks on the relevance of economic sociology have been on the microscopic level; I have illustrated this kind of relevance by asking about the different kinds of values and norms that condition economic activity. Now I turn to a more macroscopic concern, and once again I must be illustrative rather than comprehensive in my emphasis. I have chosen for illustration the kinds of repercussions throughout the social order that might be expected under conditions of long-term economic stagnation or decline – a prospect that is not unrealistic in the present phase of the world's history.

Unfortunately, our intellectual heritage has left us with little systematic knowledge about social and economic decline. Most of the scholarly literature of social and economic change concerns processes of growth. The literature on decline yields, on the one hand, a number of traditional historical treatments which are, however, devoted mainly to historical detail; and, on the other, a number of grand theories of social growth and decline, which are, however, more social-philosophical and prophetic than scientific in character.[32] In the absence of a clear body of systematic theory and empirical findings in this area, I shall have to be quite speculative about the likely social and political implications of a long period of economic stagnation or decline.

1.3.1. Structures, groups, and conflict associated with growth

Many years ago, in our collaborative work, Parsons and I took an interest in the social aspects of economic change. Like most who write on social change, however, we focussed almost exclusively on growth.[33] We were interested, moreover, in the kinds of structures that accompany

32. A number of these theories are summarized and criticized in Pitirim A. Sorokin, *Modern Historical and Social Philosophies* (New York: Dover Publications, 1963).
33. Talcott Parsons and Neil J. Smelser, *Economy and Society* (Glencoe, Ill.: The Free Press, 1956).

and facilitate growth. Building on classical writers like Adam Smith, Herbert Spencer, and Emile Durkheim as well as on contemporary theory and research on processes of social change, we stressed the importance of *structural differentiation* as a growth phenomenon. In essence our model stated that under conditions of dissatisfaction with economic production, when combined with a sense of opportunity and availability of facilities, a typical process of change unfolds. It begins with various short-term reactions to the dissatisfaction, which we termed 'symptoms of disturbance'. These gradually give way, however, to more directed attacks on the points of dissatisfaction, and the 'invention' of new, more specialized social arrangements that are, in fact, more effective as organizing bases for economic production.

Parsons and I concentrated on a single example of structural differentiation – the rise of the modern, management-dominated corporation and the well-known separation of ownership and managerial control. It is, however, possible to generalize the model of differentiation, and apply it more widely to both economy and society. That complex of changes we refer to variously as 'growth', 'development', or 'modernization' involves, above all, the growth of more differentiated roles and social structures. The economy itself produces a proliferation of more and more highly specialized occupational roles and corporate forms. Complex educational structures appear, taking over functions previously lodged in the kinship-religious complex. As we saw, the family loses a wide range of functions as a consequence of development and, as a consequence, it becomes a much more specialized institution. And it has been argued that the essence of modern religious change is in the direction of greater differentiation of religious beliefs and structures.[34]

The implications of widespread structural differentiation can be analyzed further. The appearance of more differentiated roles and structures provides a series of bases for the formation of new *groups*, including classes. The introduction of an industrial system, for example, leads to the formation of new groupings based on positions in the industrial structure – managers, workers, professionals such as engineers, for example – each of which develops expectations regarding its place in the society's status structure and its rights to political participation and influence. The same can be said for a complex

34. Talcott Parsons, 'Some Comments on the Pattern of Religious Organization in the United States', in Parsons, *Structure and Process in Modern Societies* (Glencoe, Ill: The Free Press, 1960), pp. 295-321.

educational structure, which develops its groups or estates of faculty, administrators, students, trustees, etc., all with varying degrees of consciousness and organization. While the transition from structural category (e.g., occupational role) to group membership is far from automatic, it is clear that differentiated social structures provide one of the most fundamental bases for group identification in developed societies.

The picture is made more complex by the fact that the development of new structures and groups is, above all, uneven. The appearance of new structures and new groups in one sector of society sets up pressures to change in other sectors. Responsive changes in these other sectors, in turn, ramify in various directions – including feedbacks to the sector originally considered as the leader – and further multiply the pressures to change. The image of society that emerges from this 'lead-lag' perspective is one of continuously generated and regenerated tensions, strains, contradictions, and pressures to change.

To illustrate the lead-lag perspective, let us suppose that the leading developmental sector is the economic one – though often empirically it is not – and the society in question rapidly introduces an industrial system and a concomitant expansion of the market system. Such a change is likely to generate pressures in many directions. For example, it may place pressure on the family and educational pressure to produce a higher – or at least different – quality of skills among potential recruits to the labor force. Or, again, the development of a regional and national labor market may threaten traditional sanction systems – based on ties of kinship or locality – by which individuals previously undertook their economic performances.

To take another illustration, suppose the political sector is the leading one, and the crucial change is the introduction of a mass suffrage system – a change, incidentally, that has frequently closely followed political independence in many new nations. This kind of political change may raise concerns on the part of political leaders about the qualifications of the electorate and their capacity to participate responsibly in the polity, and these concerns may generate pressure to upgrade the educational system, and, along with it, the political responsibility of the citizenry. Efforts to develop the educational system, however, may create further pressures to change, for one concomitant of increased education is a heightening of occupational expectations, and unless education is accompanied by a level of economic development, it will be difficult to sustain a population with a higher skill level; the society is likely to be faced with diverse groups of overeducated, underemployed, and politically dissatisfied citizens.

Carrying this perspective further, we may identify the following types of *conflict* that emerge in the course of economic and social development:

- Conflicts associated with the transformation of the traditional social order. Typically these conflicts have to do with the displacement of occupational (craftsman, peasant) and other (local squire, chieftain) groups, and the resistences offered to that displacement.
- Conflicts associated with the rise, legitimization, and consolidation of new groups such as capitalists, factory workers, and new types of professionals.
- Conflicts among various groups over various kinds of rewards and privileges. These may, in turn, take the form of: 1. status-conflicts, in which members of a given status group (e.g., engineers, organized labor) strive to increase wages, social respect, political bargaining position; 2. class-conflicts, in which groups organize to protest the principles on which the social rewards, especially income, are distributed. Lipset has argued that, in American history at least, status-conflicts predominate in periods of prosperity and inflation, whereas class-conflicts predominate in periods of unemployment and depression.[35]

Because all these kinds of conflicts are more or less continuously regenerated, the process of growth development evidently calls for a highly developed system of conflict-management. And while the forms of conflict-management systems that have arisen in the developed and developing countries have varied greatly in structure and effectiveness, the form that has predominated in the modern Western industrialized nations is some form of parliamentary democracy, with representation and compromise as the dominant modes of conflict-management. Furthermore, while strategies of parliamentary governments have had a diversified history, the dominant mode of political management that has emerged since the great depression of the 1930's is the pursuit of policies of economic growth, full employment, moderate inflation, and seeking compromises among the major economic and social groupings of society over the relative shares of an expanding economic base.

35. S. M. Lipset, The Sources of the Radical Right, in: Daniel Bell (ed.), *The New American Right* (New York: Criterion Books, 1955), pp. 166-233.

1.3.2. Structures, groups and conflicts, associated with stagnation or decline

In a paper this brief and tentative, I shall neither attempt to lay out all the specific parameters of a stagnating or declining economy, nor attempt to draw any formal or predictive models. Instead, I shall attempt to identify some of the probable directions of social and political change that arise under economic conditions – whether induced by the play of the market or by political control of supplies – that create a situation of high unemployment *and* serious inflation, based on higher costs and shortages of the basic materials for the economically productive sector of societies. I shall also make the debatable assumption, for purposes of analysis, that new technological advances will not be able to reverse the trend toward stagnation or decline.

In carrying out this line of speculation, one assumption in particular will inform my remarks. Growth involves *both* the increase in economic indices such as gross national product, *and* the proliferation of differentiated structures, the appearance of new groups, and the development of more complex integrative structures geared to the management of conflict. Stagnation or decline involves a distinct slowing or reversal in the movement of economic indices, *but* it cannot be expected that the major social structures and social groups generated by growth will disappear in the same – but reverse – way they appeared. They have a certain 'stickiness' because they have become the loci of the economic, political, and social interests. Regarded in this way, economic stagnation and decline leaves in its wake what might be called an 'excess capacity' of social structures and political significant groups that are very resistent to change.

1. Two likely economic consequences. First, we might review which groups in society tend to suffer under circumstances of combined inflation and depression. *Inflation* typically hurts those groups whose income is based on fixed rates of pay, changes in which are usually difficult to achieve, and which lag behind the general wage and price structure. I refer to such groups as pensioners, people on welfare, students on scholarships, those living off savings yielding fixed rates of interest, and so on. Such groups are the most visible victims of inflation. Groups that have strong bargaining power, such as some trade unions, also suffer, because in general, wages tend to lag behind prices in the current situation; but insofar as they have bargaining power they can

make up the loss more quickly than other wage sectors. Under conditions of shortages and declining economic activity, *unemployment* strikes a varied pattern of blows, depending on the precise points of constriction. Should shortages of energy continue to be a significant feature of the economic situation, unemployment would hit industries that are especially linked to and dependent upon energy sources, such as automobiles, perhaps steel, and travel and recreation. Whatever the precise pattern of unemployment and inflation, however, there is a good prospect that the effect of both on the structure of income will be *regressive*, taking a greater toll on the lower economic groups in society.

Second, insofar as the cost conditions for basic industries worsen, this constitutes, in effect, a worsening of the conditions of production, and a diminution of the economic surplus that can be devoted to other kinds of industry and activity that are not 'economically productive' in the immediate sense. Under conditions of energy and resource constriction, we should expect a relative squeeze on those kinds of industry and activity. It would perhaps be too hopeful to predict that societies would begin to dedicate less of their surplus to the wasteful military sector. It is more reasonable to expect that the pressure will be to cut back on education, medicine, welfare, and other social services we have come to value as integral parts of social-democratic systems. The productivity of modern nations has permitted them to devote their surpluses to gigantic military arsenals and gigantic welfare establisments; crises of energy and resources call into question the ability of industrial nations to continue such economic 'luxuries'.

2. Implications for stratification. One of the characteristic features of stratification systems is that various kinds of visible signs come to *symbolize* a person's position in the stratification system – styles of dress, possession of art objects, evidence of education or cultivation, location of residence, location of summer residence, and so on. It is also clear that in modern history much of the symbolization of class position is closely tied to material items. Many of these material items, moreover, are closely linked to energy: to own one's own car; to own two cars; to own two sports cars; to own a boat; to own a plane; to maintain two residences between which one travels frequently for weekends or vacations.

Sticking with the energy example – because that is the one that has been driven home so vividly in the past few years – shortages and increasing costs threaten those kinds of status symbolization. Automobiles and other forms of travel will demand a greater proportion of the family income than before, and a certain proportion of families will be forced to cut back. We may observe, in fact, that in periods of economic reversal, history plays tricks on those who made it. Having taught our citizens that the signs of status are luxury and mobility, we now learn that these signs of the proof of our worth may become increasingly unavailable to us. Under such circumstances people begin not only to feel the pressure to modify their life styles, but also to question the value of symbols that were once taken for granted. One read in the press in the winter of 1973-74 that Sundays without automobiles in many European countries constituted less of a hardship than was intially anticipated. Part of this may be due to the kind of collective pleasure that people experience when they face a crisis together. But in addition, people discovered that they were engaged in activities that were intrinsically enjoyable to them – visiting, talking, walking with the family, and so on. Such experiences sooner or later raise the question in people's minds whether the best thing to do on Sunday or any other day is to race about the countryside in an automobile. In this way *standards* of symbolization of life style begin to be brought into question.

In the longer run the changed patterns of consumption – particularly the relative decline in consumption of different groups – are likely to generate serious social discontent and conflict. Citizens will endure hardships in the name of a crisis for a certain time, but this adaptation cannot be counted on in the long run. People eventually come to feel threatened, deprived, and cheated; they begin to demand things of the society; every social group begins to feel that it is carrying too much of the sacrifice. Furthermore, the *pattern* of social conflict under conditions of restriction is different from that under conditions of expansion. With growth the pattern is more the conflict of status groups typically associated with rising expectations; it is a kind of manic, aggressive struggle to reap a larger portion of the social and economic pie, combined with a sense of expansiveness and limitlessness that gives conflict a somewhat uncontrolled character. Under conditions of static or falling expectations, however, the style of conflict differs. Groups become defensive and security-minded; they grasp what they have and resist the intrusions of others, and this gives conflict a bitter, closed character. Furthermore, they are likely to endow conflict with class overtones, raising more general questions of justice and equality, and challenging the principles underlying the distribution of the valued things of life.

The changing character of economic life under conditions of resource constriction has a further implication for social justice. With the diminution of growth and productivity rates, previously disadvantaged groups find it increasingly difficult to gain parity. An example from the recent history of higher education in American society will make the point. Late in the 1960's, as part of the political turmoil in American society, various minority groups (black and Mexican Americans, for example) and women became more conscious politically of the enduring patterns of exclusion from faculty positions in institutions of higher education. Out of this increased consciousness developed an increased political pressure to recruit from among these groups. But precisely at the moment when the promise of access was increasing, the growth rate in higher education slowed, leaving few positions open for candidates of any sort, and, of course, continuing the pattern of disadvantage intact. It is easier to realize equality of opportunity when a system is growing and new positions are being created. Sociologists like Duncan and Blau, in their research on patterns of social mobility in recent American history,[36] found that much upward mobility is accounted for by the creation of new occupational positions in the process of relatively steady economic advance. It follows that should the growth rate of the economy slow, the effects on rates of social mobility would be adverse. Add to this the fact that in periods of unemployment the unskilled, marginal laboring groups experience the highest rates of unemployment – witness the examples of the American minorities, especially blacks, and the migrant workers in various European countries. One discovers again the regressive effects associated with a slowing rate of economic growth, unless active efforts – usually by national governments – are made to counter such effects.

3. A possible cultural impact? Perhaps the most fundamental – but at the same time the most difficult to predict – impact of long-term stagnation and decline is a cultural one. Such conditions may well cause us to question a wide range of cultural values which have become almost second nature to us in the past several centuries. These values, deriving originally from what has come to be known as the 'Protestant Ethic' – but now spread world-wide – include the following:

- The valuation of *freedom* of man to exploit his natural environment.
- The valuation of *work, hard work*, for its own sake.

36. Peter Blau and Otis Dudley Duncan, *The American Occupational Structure* (New York: Wiley, 1967).

- The valuation of *mastery, achievement,* and *personal ambition* as desirable human qualities.
- The valuation of *rationality,* especially scientific rationality, in the organization of economic and social life.

It seems that the headlong and mindless worship of these values constitutes a large part of the reason we now face some of our environmental imbalances and threatened shortages of resources. These values have contributed directly to the exploitation, the spoilage, and ultimately the exhaustion of the environment. It is again one of the ironies of history that after centuries of struggle these values have conquered the world, and at precisely the moment of victory, the values themselves have proved to be archaic and outmoded, even burdensome and dysfunctional.

The cumulative impact of stagnation punctuated by crises of supply is to create a sort of cultural confusion, a cultural vacuum. We may become haunted by many questions: What have we been living for? What is of value if these values are not? Where are we to turn if we cannot turn to these values? At the same time we are such victims of the values of rationalistic mastery of the universe that we find it difficult to think of solutions in terms other than those suggested by these values. Yet the same values, we may be made increasingly aware, will not be the appropriate ones for a situation of crisis and stagnation; to apply them blindly would be simply to worsen the situation we have created for ourselves. I am not suggesting that there is not a technological aspect to the problem of warding off a period of economic stagnation or decline. But I would suggest that the worship of the system of values that gives technology such a central role may be inappropriate in the future, and that greater emphasis will be given to more humanistic values that have fallen by the wayside as science and technology have conquered the world. And is it not only natural for values to drift in the humanistic direction? I mean here 'natural' in the sense that it is evidently the adaptive thing to do in man's constant struggle for survival when those values – scientific and technological values – that have helped him survive so well into the twentieth century reach their limits as adaptive devices.

4. Some possible political consequences. I might conclude this section by speculating that the sorts of economic and social changes I have envisioned as arising from resource constriction and economic stagnation will pose a severe test for individualistic democracy as a political and legal system. This test, moreover, promises to have two facets:

The first concerns the volume of conflict that societies will be called upon to accommodate. If what I have said about the impact of declining expectations is correct, there will be few groups and classes who will not be discontented and who will not express that discontent in the form of demands on the political system. And if what I have said about the regressive effects of resource constriction – and its effects on social justice – we should expect an overload of deprivation, experienced especially by those at the lower end of the stratification system.

Two of the conditions of stable democracy are that its internal conflicts take place within a framework of general consensus about the legitimacy of the system of government, and that the level of conflict remains below that which the mediating political processes can sustain. If either of these conditions fails to be met, the political system itself is endangered, and there arises a temptation on the part of political authorities to rely on methods more repressive than the arts of mediation and compromise to deal with internal conflict. To say this is by no means to predict that heretofore democratic societies will move in a totalitarian direction; democratic institutions have their own kind of resiliency. But they will be tempted to move in that direction, mainly because they will be confronted with conflict of a magnitude and bitterness that will contrast with the relative political quiescence of various social groups during the past quarter-century.

The second facet concerns a probable threat to institutions associated with the system of private property – institutions that permit individuals great freedom in acquiring, using, and disposing of economically valuable resources and commodities. These institutions do not require plenty; they operate, like all of human life, in the realm of scarcity, since most resources have never been free. But when scarcity turns to shortage – that is to say, when the unavailability of resources becomes a matter that affects the functioning of a society as a *whole*, then the society's interest in those resources necessarily becomes a *collective* interest. Certainly that has been the case with various fuels; they invariably will become the subject of more collectivized regulation at the national level. Indeed, logic dictates that collective interest in such resources should extend to the international level. Once again, I venture no predictions as to the exact pattern that the collectivization of interest in resources will take. Many options are available – nationalization, international coordination, and regulation of various sorts. But I am suggesting that the increasing role of government that accompanied the expansion and increasing complexity of the industrial democracies will continue in the same direction as these democracies suffer from constricted resources and slowing rates of growth. It is a final example of the principle that reversals in economic fortunes are not accompanied by parallel reversals in the social and political sectors; indeed, trends in those sectors – such as the collectivization of interest in economic life – may move faster in the same direction than they have moved in the advanced stages of economic growth.

1.4. Economics, sociology and questions of public policy

Continuing his definition of economics, Samuelson noted that economics 'analyzes the costs and benefits of improving patterns of resource allocation'.[37] In the sub-field of economics known as welfare economics, this kind of analysis has been carried very far. In recent years, welfare economists, taking advantage of increasingly sophisticated logical and mathematical tools, have generated a series of complex formal statements on the relations between public policy and the preferences of members of a society.[38] On the more empirical side, they have generated models for assessing, for example, different feudal and capitalist systems of ownership and production,[39] and they have made detailed assessments of medical and educational systems, patterns of taxation, military conscription, and other institutions and policies of public concern.[40]

By and large, welfare economists have traced only the *economic* consequences of different institutional arrangements and public policies, and, among those consequences, only those that are measurable by changes in money income or wealth. Within a framework of economic sociology, however, this basis for assessing policy is extremely limited. As I have indicated, economic sociology brings a host of additional variables to bear on the analysis of economic activity – variables such as religious values, family structure, social stratification and political structure. Furthermore, since it regards economic activity as embedded in a complex of non-economic variables – affecting and being affected by

37. *Economics, op. cit.*, p. 3.
38. For a survey of these technical developments, see Armatya K. Sen, *Collective Choice and Social Welfare* (San Francisco: Holden-Day, 1970).
39. L.S. Shapley and Martin Shubik, 'Ownership and the Production Function', in *Quarterly Journal of Economics,* Vol. 81 (1967), pp. 88-111.
40. For a survey of such analyses, see James M. Buchanan and D. Tollison (eds.), *Theory of Public Choice* (Ann Arbor: University of Michigan Press, 1972).

them – it follows that any set of institutional arrangements or policy decisions will have implications not only for economic welfare, but for other types of 'welfare' as well – social justice, family security, emotional well-being, and so on. To press this point further, it should be pointed out that a more nearly complete assessment of the consequences of social policies should systematically take into account the additional variables and perspectives provided by the sociological framework.

That point seems unobjectionable, but to it must be added a series of qualifications:

1. The knowledge generated by research in economic sociology is frequently lacking in adequacy, and is correspondingly limited as a basis for assessing or predicting the consequences of any given policy. Consider a specific example. In a carefully-conducted piece of research, Marris analyzed the impact of a slum-clearance project in Lagos. Presumably the project was justified on economic grounds – that the economic welfare of the inhabitants would be increased via the improvement of their residences and their neighborhood. Marris found, however, that the projected improvements not only disrupted patterns of family interaction, such as visiting, but eroded the system of employment, credit, and mutual aid that was patterned on and bolstered by the network of kinship loyalties.[41] Put in welfare terms, Marris' findings suggest that the project involved a cost from the standpoint of family security, and this constitutes a basis for a policy recommendation opposite to that suggested by economic welfare conditions. Now, Marris' research seemed to establish fairly clearly that those costs were incurred in the particular situation he studied. But, equally clearly, his findings are not generalizable in any simple way. In other settings, characterized by other kinds of kinship structures, such a cost in family security might not have been exacted by the razing of a neighborhood and the transfer of its residents. Moreover, the knowledge based on such research is correspondingly limited as a basis for assessing the consequences of relevant policy decisions.

2. Different kinds of gains and costs are, in many cases, not comparable. To continue with the same example, suppose that our knowledge of both the gains in economic welfare and the costs in family security is completely adequate. Even under this hypothetical condition, the implications for policy are not clear, because we have no way of

41. Peter Marris, *Family and Social Change in an African City: A Study of Rehousing in Lagos* (London: Routledge and Kegan Paul, 1961).

unambiguously measuring both kinds of welfare by comparable units or, for that matter, no way of deciding unambiguously which kinds of welfare – economic or family security – is more important or compelling as a guide to policy decisions. Given those circumstances, it is only possible for policymakers to take the various welfare considerations 'into account' in some qualitative way.

3. Even greater difficulties are encountered when there is lack of consensus on what constitutes a cost or a benefit. Still remaining with the slum-clearance example, it might be argued that we have sufficient consensus of our values concerning economic welfare and income redistribution that the slum-clearance project can be regarded as a gain in welfare. But what about the criteria for assessing family security? These are clearly more ambiguous and subject to dispute. Some would argue that the extended kin network is the basis for family security, while others might argue that family security is better secured in the individuated nuclear family unit, particularly if that family is situated in comfortable residential surroundings. If the former argument is believed, then the slum-clearance project would involve a cost of family security; if the latter, then it would involve a gain. The assessment of gains and costs, in short, is a function of the criteria applied to empirical changes as well as of the objective characteristics of the empirical changes themselves. And insofar as there is lack of consensus on those criteria, unambiguous assessment of costs and gains cannot be made.

The promise of directly applying the knowledge generated by economics and economic sociology to policy decisions, then, is not especially promising at the present time, because of the qualifications just enumerated. One final point might be made, however. One of the items that should be on the future agenda of research for economic sociology might well be to study how policy decisions are made *empirically* under different kinds of conditions – that is, when knowledge is reliable, when different and incomparable yardsticks must be relied upon to assess policies, and when there is limited or no consensus on the criteria for assessing gains and costs. Such research might lead to a better understanding of the role of magical thinking, cliches, slogans, and other non-rational factors in the generation of policy decisions. The sociologist is certainly equipped to undertake such research, and the findings emerging from it might well throw light on the quality of policy-decisions by studying the decision-making *process* itself as well as the empirical consequences that subsequently unfold.

2. Economic sociology or sociological economics?

The theory of social exchange and its bearing on neoclassical economics; towards an interdisciplinary conception of society

Tjerk Huppes

2.1. Introduction

In this paper economists are invited to enlarge the scope of their discipline with the aid of sociology. Taking as a point of departure both neoclassical economics and the theory of social exchange, an interdisciplinary conception of society is developed.

The neoclassical mainstream in economics is subject to a number of well-known limitations, emphasized by neokeynesians, institutionalists, neomarxists and others. In their alternatives, the world of neoclassical economics is refuted. In contrast, our effort may be conceived of as an attempt to reconcile man as a social actor with man as a homo economicus. An ambitious effort indeed, considering the non-sociological character of neoclassical economics. Thus Hans Albert tells us that:

> 'Wenn auch der soziologische Charakter ökonomischer Probleme relativ leicht festzustellen ist, so kann man doch nicht sagen, dass die theoretische Ökonomie bisher für ihre Problemlösungen grossen Nutzen aus den Forschungsergebnissen der allgemeinen Sociologie... gezogen hätte. Das ist auch nicht zu erwarten, solange der neoklassische Denkstil die Theoriebildung beherrscht, der die ökonomische Analyse in Richtung auf eine möglichst weitgehende Abstraktion von sozialen Tatbeständen lenkt... Die theoretische Nationalökonomie neoklassische Stils scheint also in ganz merkwürdiger Weise sociologische Problemstellungen mit relativ soziologiefreien Problemlösungen zu verbinden. Sie scheint gegen das Eindringen soziologischer und sozialpsychologischer Erkentnisse immun zu sein'.[1]

1. Hans Albert, Modell Platonismus, Der neoklassische Stil des ökonomischen Denkens in kritischer Beleuchtung, in: E. Topitsch, *Logik der Sozialwissenschaften*, 1965, p. 406.

The neoclassical paradigm may be characterized as utilitarianistic, rationalistic and atomistic. Rationally calculating economic subjects act in their own interest. Because of the atomistic structure of society they do not harm each other. On the contrary, their acting in this way brings prosperity for all.[2] 'Private vice makes public benefit'.[3] Assuming diminishing marginal utility and rising costs, the market mechanism generates a general state of equilibrium. In the neoclassical world harmony figures largely.

Designed by Walras (1870) and Marshall (1890), refined by Pareto (1920), interrupted by Keynes (1936), the general equilibrium model still dominates post-war neoclassical economics (Mead, Samuelson, Solow, SMAC and others). Even modern theories of production and income distribution stick to the assumption of perfect competition. The oligopolistic firm for instance does not lend itself to integration into macro-models. Moreover, the institutional structure is considered exogeneous and non-variable: a datum. Thus power and conflict remain concealed in neoclassical economics.[4] Social change and its bearing on economic variables is abstracted from.[5]

2. Nothwithstanding his elaborate style, Max Weber has given a lucid exposition of the (neo) classical 'ideal type': 'Die Nationalökonomie war... von Anfang an... eingegliedert in die mächtige Einheit der naturrechtlichen und rationalistischen Weltanschauung des achtzehnten Jahrhunderts. Aber die Eigenart jener Weltanschauung mit ihrem optimistischen Glauben an die theoretische und praktische Rationalisierbarkeit des Wirklichen wirkte wesentlich insofern, als sie hinderte, dass der *problematische* Charakter jenes als selbstverständlich vorausgesetzten Gesichtspunktes entdeckt wurde... Die mächtigen Rückwirkungen dieser glaubenfrohen Stimmung des naturalistischen Monismus auf die ökonomischen Disziplinen, hielt... die Nationalökonomie davon ab, das Verhältnis von Begriff und Wirklichkeit in vollem Umfang deutlich zu erkennen... Die Wirtschaftstheorie... bietet uns ein *Idealbild* der Vorgänge aus dem Gütermarkt bei tauschwirtschaftlicher Gesellschaftsorganisation, freier Konkurrenz und streng rationellem Handeln. Dieses Gedankenbild vereinigt bestimmte Beziehungen und Vorgänge des historischen Lebens zu einem in sich widerspruchlosen Kosmos *gedachter* Zusammenhänge. Inhaltlich trägt diese Konstruktion den Charakter einer Utopie an sich die durch *gedankliche* Steigerung bestimmter Elementen der Wirklichkeit gewonnen ist'.
Max Weber, *Soziologie, Weltgeschichtliche Analysen, Politik,* 1967. p. 230 et. seq.

3. H. de Mandeville. *The fable of the bees,* 1706.

4. In Marxian economics power and conflict play a central role. In contrast to neoclassical economics there is no room for harmony. According to Marx 'orthodox' economics are not aware of 'the socially conditioned character of general economic categories and relationships'. They regard 'the given social arrangements as natural, harmonious and eternal'. D. Horowitz (ed.) *Marx and Modern Economics,* 1968, p. 14.

5. Institutional economics (Galbraith, Myrdal, Heilbroner, Gruchy and others) may be conceived of as an attempt towards an integration of economic and social life. A summary of its specific features has been given by K.W. Kapp, 'In defense of institutional economics', *Swedish Journal of Economics,* 1968.

The sociological concept of society is altogether different. Man as a social actor belongs to various groups. Internalized norms enable him to participate in social life. He conforms, plays varying roles, occupies a rank in the status hierarchy, and so on. His sense of identity is derived from his orientation towards others. Interaction, norms, roles and institutions, structure the sociological conception of society. Social change, power and conflict, figure largely and it is precisely these phenomena that neoclassical economics does not deal with. Heilbroner:

'The answer I wish to give is not to denigrate what economics has done. It is to stress what it has failed to do... The light of economics only seems to work when the machinery of the social system is turning over smoothly, whereas any failure in the social mechanism shortcircuits the beam that economics throws'.[6]

Man as a social actor remains outside the sphere of economic abstraction or is only dealt with marginally. In itself there is no objection to this. No science without abstraction; each discipline involves leaving certain aspects of reality out of consideration. However, in many problems economists are confronted with, sociological variables play an important part. In these cases an interdisciplinary perspective is desirable.

Desirable indeed, but not easy. For one thing, within the field of sociology, there are all sorts of different theories and definitions concerning the subject matter of this multi-paradigmatic discipline. Economics present a more uniform picture. In any handbook, it is practically always the elements of scarcity, choice and the scale of preference that determine the concept of economic behaviour. Sociological textbooks are less homogeneous. Max Weber is often taken as a point of departure. In his view, sociology should focus primarily on the subjective meanings that human actors attach to their actions in their mutual orientations within specific social-historical contexts. Behaviour devoid of such meaning, Weber argued, falls outside the purview of sociology. Alternative approaches, however, are numerous. Wallace[7] distinguishes no less than eleven, restricting himself moreover to what in some circles is indicated by the term 'bourgeois sociology'.

Less detailed is the triad of theories, respectively highlighting consensus, exchange and conflict. An interdisciplinary approach thus entails the complication that one must choose one from several sociological conceptualizations. By what criterion?

6. R.L. Heilbroner, 'On the limited relevance of economics', in D. Bell and I. Kristol, eds. *Capitalism today,* 1972, p. 81, et. seq.
7. W.L. Wallace, *Sociological Theory,* 1969.

Both economists and sociologists study human behaviour. It is only the perspectives in which this behaviour is placed – the conceptual frameworks within which it is interpreted – that diverge.[8] To the economist, the consumption of marijuana is consumer behaviour, in which preferences, choice, and scarcity play a part. A sociologist, however, will designate this behaviour as deviant, or, if it happens to be part of religious practices, as normative behaviour. Human behaviour thus becomes economic behaviour or social behaviour depending on one's point of view. In itself it is neither the one nor the other.[9]

The same applies to the various approaches within the field of sociology. A functionalist's view of society will differ from that of a neomarxist, and it is hard to reduce both conceptions to the same denominator.[10]

Fortunately there happens to be a school of thought within sociology working with a similar paradigm as neoclassical economics. Meant is the theory of exchange, it most distinghuished representatives being: George C. Homans and Peter M. Blau. In extending classical economics sociologically, it thus stands to reason that preference has been given to the theory of social exchange. Our attention will be primarily focussed on Homans, the first to bring the concept of social exchange into prominence.[11] His exchange theory will be confronted with the neoclassical – more in particular the Paretian – equilibrium model. In this approach economic and social key concepts will figure as simular phenomena. In the first place we will compare norms and prices, in the second place the process of social control and the market mechanism, and finally the allocation of power and the income distribution. Thus the interdisciplinary conception is taking shape. After including conflict and social change the present problem of inflation will serve as an illustration.

8. Cf. N.J. Smelser's lucid exposition in his *Sociology: An Introduction,* 1967, p. 3 et seq.
9. A more comprehensive example including other disciplines is provided by H. Zetterberg, *On Theory and Verification in Sociology,* 1965, p. 24.
10. Nevertheless P.L. van de Berghe makes an attempt. See his 'Dialetic and Functionalistic: Toward a theoretical synthesis, *American Sociological Review,* Oct. 1963.
11. In social psychology exchange theory has first been developed by J.W. Thibault and H.H. Kelley, *The Social Psychology of Groups,* 1959.

2.2. Homans en Pareto

'To Benny, who made me a Paretian'. These are Homans' words in his book *An Introduction to Pareto*. Benny is Bernard de Voto, who founded a library at Harvard which has borne his name ever since.

Particulary Homans' *Social Behaviour: Its Elementary Forms*, in which he reveals himself as an exchange theorist, shows considerable affinity to Pareto's optimum theorem. In this book the economic equilibrium model is applied to social relations.

Pareto drew a sharp distinction between rational or logical behaviour – the subject matter of economics – and irrational or nonlogical behaviour – the aspect with which sociology is concerned. According to Pareto the actor behaves rationally if both he and an objective outsider arrive at the same conclusion as to the means of attaining a certain end. Irrational behaviour springs from not directly observable feelings, subconscious impulses and other psychological variables. Religious convictions, moral values, political ideologies, but most sociological theories as well, have their roots in the latter. To Pareto they are rationalizations – derivations – merely serving to justify self-interest. They obscure the basically irrational motives – residues – which underlie them.

The irrational element in human behaviour vexed Pareto in no small measure. He became more and more convinced, that the development of society is mainly determined by residues and derivations. Embittered and desillusioned he carried on a fierce controversy with the Italian Government who rejected his liberal ideas, based on his optimum theorem. His resentment was carried to such lenghts that he came to embrace fascism of which however, he was only to know the beginnings.

Pareto's main importance lies no doubt in the field of economics. Mannheim's sociology of knowledge supplies a more acceptable explanation of what Pareto indicated as derivations. His residues have been superseded by Freud's psychoanalysis.

And what about Homans? His theory of exchange may be seen as an attempt to translate that part of human behaviour, so hard to stomach for Pareto, into economic categories. Sociology and economics are reduced to the same denominator:

> '... we recognize no line between sociology and psychology or, indeed, between sociology and the other social sciences such as economics'.[12]

12. G.C. Homans, *Fundamental Social Processes*, 1967, p. 32.

Before turning to the content of Homans' exchange theory, the similarity between his conception of social reality and the neoclassical paradigm will be discussed.

Utilitarianism.[13] In economics the consumer chooses between alternative goods. By means of exchange he satisfies his wants. Exchange takes place only when both parties involved think it will be to their advantage. Self-interest is the criterion. Homans' argument with respect to the social actor runs along the same lines. The choice is one between alternative interactions. Interaction assumes exchange. The satisfaction which both parties experience in a social relationship – social rewards – should exceed the effort, or the satisfaction attainable in alternative relationships – social costs. Social relationship will not persist, i.e. the exchange is discontinued, unless all parties involved are making a profit. Social behaviour, like economic behaviour is a function of its pay-offs.

Rationalism.[14] The exchange relation in economics is governed by rational, calculating behaviour. Consumer as well as employer maximize; the one his utilities, the other his profits. In Homans' conception social behaviour is rational as well. That is to say, if one extends the notion of rationality sufficiently. Subconscious motives too play a part in determining human behaviour, and Homans does not want to leave them out of consideration. In fact, he eliminates the distinction between rational and irrational behaviour; Pareto's basis for the division of labour between economics and sociology. Not without difficulties though.

By including subconscious, nonobservable motives, Homans notion of rational behaviour becomes rather meaningless and tautological. Any kind of behaviour may be interpreted as rational. In his more recent work Homans solves the problem by asserting: 'For us, words like rational and irrational are good words to shy away from'.[15]

13. Utilitarianism has its roots in Epicurius' hedonism. The utilitarian philosophers Jeremy Bentham and John Stuart Mill, elaborating the 'pain-pleasure principle' have strongly influenced classical economics.

14. Rationalism dates back to the Enlightenment (Aufklärung) of the eighteenth century. Rational behaviour would contribute to the interest of everybody through the emergence of a 'natural-order' – a secularized conception of the harmony of creation. Rationalism and utilitarianism are closely related. Bentham and Mill represent both schools of thought.

15. G.C. Homans, *Ibid.*, p. 41.

Boulding tries to break the deadlock as follows: 'The distinction between rational and irrational behavior lies in the degree of self-consciousness and the stability of the images involved rather than in any distinction of the principle of optimum'. K. Boulding, *Conflict and Defense,* 1962, p. 151. Also cf. Katona's distinction between 'genuine decision making' and 'habitual behavior'. 'The main alternative to problem-solving is not whimsical or

Atomism.[16] Finally, Homans' concept is atomistic as well. Social behaviour is individualistically orientated. Altruism, in Homans view, is a manifestation of egocentric behaviour. The concern with fellow-man clearly leads to rewards, otherwise why bother? To Homans, fellow-man is as it were 'dehumanized', he merely serves as a means to an end.

'... no new principles are required to explain social behaviour that were not needed to explain how a man acts when he is alone with the physical environment'.[17]

A conclusion, not many sociologists would endorse. Social interaction is dominated by the same laws as those governing the interaction between a man and his physical environment. In this too, Homans' exchange theory corresponds to the neoclassical view. His sociology lends itself admirably to an interdisciplinary perspective.

The theory of social exchange is hardly, if at all, known to economists. Those versed in economics, however, will find it quite easy to understand. Now, one sees man as a social actor behaving similary to a consumer maximizing his utilities, then again one finds exchange relations operating in accordance with the law of comparative costs, or, differences in rank and power being explained in a way reminding one of the theory of income distribution. More about this in the next section.

impulsive behavior (which was considered the major example of 'irrational' behavior by nineteenth century philosophers). When genuine decision making does not take place, habitual behavior is the most usual occurence: people act as they have acted before under simular circumstances, without deliberating and choosing; George Katona, *Rational Behavior and Economic Behavior,* 1959, reprinted in H.H. Kassarjian en T.S. Robertson (eds.), *Perspectives in Consumer Behavior,* 1968.

In business economics the concept of 'objective' rationality has been abondoned after the introduction of the behavioural approach by J.G. March and H.A. Simon, *Organizations* (1958) and R.M. Cyert and J.G. March, *A behavioral theory of the firm* (1963). The actor's 'definition of the situation' is what determines his behaviour; a view, not unfamiliar to sociologists: W.I. Thomas and F. Znaniencki, *The Polish Peasant in Europe and America,* 1918-1920, p. 68. Business economics has oriented itself towards interdisciplinary views to a marked degree. General economics has lagged behind in this respect.

16. The atomistic conception of society is bound up with the name of Gottfried Wilhelm von Leibniz, the most important precursor of the Enlightenment. In Leibniz' view, society is made up of independent individuals (monades), who strive for self-realization (a higher degree of consciousness). Progress is being served, as God has established harmony among all monades (harmonie préétablie). The 'triad' of utilitarianism, rationalism and atomism constitute a coherent whole.

17. G.C. Homans, *Ibid.*, p. 32.

2.3. Homans' conceptual apparatus

So far Homans has published two sociological standard works: *The Human Group* (1950) and *Social Behaviour: its Elementary Forms* (1961). In *The Human Group* a theoretical system is derived from a number of empirical generalizations. Homans criticizes functionalism because it lacks the inductive basis without which theory construction is pointless. Parsons' big abstractions may serve as a taxonomy, but they hardly furnish any explanations. In starting at the bottom, i.e. at the level of directly observable behaviour, Homans seeks to offer an alternative.

'The great point is to climb down from the big words of social science, at least as far as common-sense observation. Then, if we wish, we can start climbing up again, but this time with a ladder we can depend on'.[18]

According to Homans social behaviour may be divided into four basic categories: activity, interaction, sentiments and norms. Terms whose meaning each of us more or less senses. More difficult to grasp are 'the external system' and 'the internal system', which complete his conceptual apparatus.

'We shall not go far wrong if... we think of the external system as group behaviour that enables the group to survive in its environment and think of the internal system as group behaviour that is an expression of the sentiments towards one another developed by the members of the group in the course of their life together'.[19]

These six concepts are all Homans needs for his theory. With material from five case-studies he developes his empirical generalizations. For example: if the frequency of interaction between two or more persons increases, the degree of their liking for one another will increase, and vice versa. Generalizations like these enable him to construct a general deductive system.

Homans' ideas on social exchange do not play a prominent part in *The Human Group*. The book is mentioned to make his later work stand out in relief. It is in *Social Behaviour* that Homans develops his theory of social exchange. Before the concept of exchange can become operative, however, he first has to adapt his conceptual apparatus. The four basic categories – activity, interaction, sentiments and norms – are reduced to one by regarding them as sub-categorizations of 'human activity or

18. G.C. Homans, *The Human Group*, 1950, p. 13.
19. *Ibid.*, p. 109-110.

behaviour'. Explicitly behaviouristic definitions are adopted. Thus sentiments are:

'activities that the members of a particular verbal or symbolic community say are signs of the attitudes and feelings a man takes towards another man or other men... Sentiments are not internal states of an individual any more than words are. They are not inferred from overt behaviour; they are overt behaviour and so are directly observable'.[20]

Norms are defined as:

'Statements made by a number of members of a group, not necessary all of them, that the members ought to behave in a certain way in certain circumstances'.[21]

By this redefinition all Homans' 'activities' have become observable. It doesn't follow, however, that they are quantifiable. This too is necessary. Social transactions should have a common denominator if the theory of exchange is to have a solid foundation. This problem plays hardly any part in economics, where money is taken as unit of account. Commodities are comparable after multiplying quantity and price. Money facilitates economic exchange.

In the case of social exchange things are more complicated. It is especially hard to reduce the various sentiments exchanged during an interaction to a common unit of account. Yet Homans claims that both quantity and value can be distinguished as dimensions of all social behaviour. 'Quantity' is related to the number of activities per unit of time; and 'value' is defined as the degree of positive or negative reinforcement of a unit of activity, i.e. rewards minus costs. Rewards, e.g. social approval, are regarded as positive values; costs as negative values. By the latter Homans understands both the efforts to gain rewards during interaction and the forgone rewards of alternative interactions which have been forsaken. His notion of social costs is comparable to the absolute and/or comparative costs in economics; or, from the consumer's point of view, to the price charged for a commodity. Rewards correspond to the revenues of a firm or to the satisfaction a consumer derives from a commodity.

Homans further assumes that rewards tend to diminish when interaction is repeated, whereas costs will increase. It is not difficult to recognize the economic laws of diminishing marginal utility and of

20. G.C. Homans, *Social Behaviour: Its Elementary Forms,* 1961, p. 33.
21. *Ibid.*, p. 46.

diminishing returns (rising costs). Although Homans does not explicitly formulate any conditions of maximization, he does mention both a diminishing 'psychic profit' (rewards minus costs) when there is frequent interaction, and a state of equilibrium attainable in social relations.

Not only the four basic categories of social behaviour are subjected to a revision in *Social Behaviour*; the 'external system' too is reinterpreted.

Homans:

'The kind of things we have called givens... are the same as what I called in my earlier book the external system. I now think this is too prententious a term and suggests what is not true... If the word givens... (does not) suit the readers's taste, let him try some other phrase like parameter or boundary conditions, the boundary being the arbitrary and imaginary line dividing elementary social behaviour from what, for the purposes in hand, we choose to consider its physical and social environment in time and space'.[22]

Thus the external system has become what economists would call a datum or exogeneous variable. The internal system is studied 'ceteris paribus'.

A last difference between *Social Behaviour* and *The Human Group* should be mentioned. The empirical generalizations of the earlier work have disappeared. A number of propositions derived from behavioural psychology have taken their place. For example: 'the more often a man has, in the recent past, received a rewarding activity from another, the less valuable any further unit of that activity becomes to him'.

It is interesting to notice that Homans by introducing his propositions, undermines the inductive base of his theory. His theory of exchange is built up on a number of behaviouristic assumptions. Hypotheses about social life are deduced and confronted with empirical data. Homans scientific method has become similar to the one applied in the modern neoclassical theories of production and income distribution.

In the foregoing Homans' conceptual apparatus has been reviewed. Now it is time to examine his explanation of a number of dominant sociological concepts.

22. *Ibid.*, p. 230.

2.4. Norms and social control

Eccentrics, fools, eager beavers and grumblers; one may meet them all in social life. Nevertheless they are exceptions. Usually people behave 'normally' and it seems necessary that they do so. Deviant behaviour is not tolerated.

To those who pause to reflect, this must indeed seem remarkable, implying as it does that people are not at liberty to do as they like. At least not permanently. Diverging behaviour eventually leads to desintegration, not only of the group, but of its members as well. Normative behaviour is a 'conditio sine qua non' for man's social existence. By social control we maintain the identity of our country, our home, our personality and even our science.[23] This does not imply, by the way, that social control is always experienced as a constraint or as a restriction of one's liberty. On the contrary, conforming man may be hardly aware of a thing like social control. He takes conformity for granted in the same way a fish takes water for granted, without realizing that life outside is impossible.

Homans view of social control is based on his concept of social exchange:

> 'Control is the process by which, if a man departs from his present degree of obedience to a norm, his behaviour is brought back toward that degree... control can be effective only when that degree of obedience is the one that produces the greatest amount of satisfaction of the man's sentiments possible under the existing state of the social system, so that any departure whatever from the degree brings a decrease in satisfaction, a net punishment'.[24]

If social control is effective throughout the group, Homans refers to it as a state of equilibrium. Equilibrium exists when all group members have achieved a maximum level of satisfaction. Homans concedes that it would be difficult to establish whether each member has indeed achieved his maximum. Nevertheless, if such is the case, deviant behaviour will be brought into line. The non-conformist exchanges on the basis of norms different from those prevailing within the group and as a result his rate of interaction decreases. In economic terms: he rejects the role of pricetaker, which places him outside the market (assuming perfect

23. Cf. Kuhn's description of natural science as a self-preserving system in which social control plays an important part. Th. S. Kuhn, *The Structure of Scientific Revolution,* 1962. His view is applied to economics by Benjamin Ward, *What is wrong with economics,* 1972.
24. G.C. Homans, *The Human Group,* 1950, p. 298.

competition). His rewards will diminish and this in turn compels him to conform.

What strikes one immediately is the tautological nature of Homans' argument. By defining group equilibrium as a state of maximum satisfaction and, moreover, by assuming that every member will tend to obtain as many rewards as possible, it is only natural that conformity is maintained.

With respect to his utilitarianistic concept of social man, Homans is nevertheless consistent. It is in one's own interest not to fall out of line. The individual motivation to refrain from deviant behaviour exists, even without other group members exerting pressure.

Relevant to the interdisciplinary approach yet to be designed are the striking similarities between Homans and the realm of neoclassical economics. Homans' state of equilibrium, for instance, shows resemblance to Pareto's optimum, be it that in the latter it is economic commodities that are at stake and not social rewards. Pareto optimality arises from leaving the allocation of the factors of production to the market mechanism. The satisfaction of wants will then achieve its maximum level. A similar equilibrium, dealing with the satisfaction of wants in the sociological sense of word, is described by Homans.

Norms and prices thus prove to be familiar phenomena.Norms arise from interaction. That is from exchange transactions through which the supply and demand of social rewards meet and crystallize into norms. An authority imposing norms is superfluous. In the process of continual interaction a group will find the normative behaviour which provides the maximum level of rewards automatically. Assuming perfect competition, prices are generated in the same way. No one has power,[25] yet everyone casts his vote. The collective curves of demand and supply determine the equilibrium price. An optimal allocation of the productive resources emerges without anyone controlling prices. Thus both economically and sociologically the group optimum is attained. In a state of equilibrium market prices as well as 'market' norms are accepted by pricetakers and conformists. Every deviation results in less than the maximum attainable.

Nothwithstanding the criticisms which can be made,[26] Homans'

25. Homans does furnish an explanation of the power phenomenon. Power, however, is not a necessary attribute in exercising social control.

26. E.g. B. Abrahamsson, 'Homans on Exchange: Hedonism Revived', *American Journal of Sociology*, Sept. 1970.

theory opens up interesting perspectives for an interdisciplinary approach and although the picture of Homans is still incomplete, the first steps towards a sociological-economic view of society may now be taken.

2.5. The interdisciplinary conception I

On a much wider scale than economists have been accustomed to, human behaviour may be regarded as exchange behaviour. Not only goods and services are exchanged but also social rewards. Both prices and norms are established by exchange which they regulate in turn. The relation 'market mechanism-prices' is comparable to the relation 'social control-norms'.

Under 'laissez-faire' conditions it is even possible to postulate the evolvement of a state of equilibrium. All exchange traffic is then regulated optimally. The economic and social system supply most of what people most want. Prices and norms are accepted by everyone.

It is only one small though extremely important step further to conceive of prices as norms expressed in money and of the market mechanism as a form of social control. Hans Albert supports this view:

'Jedenfalls ist das Problem des Funktionierens von Märkten im Sinne sozialer Beziehungsnetze ohne Kontrolle durch eine zentrale Führung ein wichtiger allgemeines soziologisches Problem, und der Markt, der uns zuerst einzufallen pflegt, wenn dieses Wort benutzt wird: der Markt sogenannter wirtschaftlicher Güter und Dienstleistungen ist ein Spezialfall, wenn auch ohne Zweifel ein ausserordentlich bedeutsamer'.[27]

According to Albert Adam Smith's invisible hand may be interpreted as social control:

'Es dürfte kaum übertrieben sein zu behaupten, dass in Adam Smiths Konzeption der 'unsichtbaren Hand' eigentlich eine kybernetische Idee der sozialen Kontrolle steckt, die ihre Bedeutung auch dann behält, wenn man sie aus ihrem teilweise metaphysisch-ideologischen Hintergrund herauslöst und vor der mehr oder weniger normativen Spekulation über die Optimalität der dadurch zustandegekommen Ordnung der sozialen Geschehens abstrahiert, einer Spekulation, deren letzte Ausläufer in der Wohlfahrtsökonomie zu finden sind'.[28]

27. Hans Albert, *Marktsoziologie und Entscheidungslogik*, 1967, p. 395.
28. *Ibid.*, p. 400.

So it is essential to the interdisciplinary conception that:
- economic goods and social rewards
- prices and norms
- the market mechanism and social control

should be treated alike. Some examples are in order.

Economic goods and social rewards. The price one charges to a friend will be less than the price charged to a third party. Social rewards – proofs of friendship – compensate for the lower price. The rate of exchange deviates from the market price; yet the transaction takes place without either party feeling deprived. Apparently both economic goods and social rewards yield utilities; both satisfy wants. In exchange transaction they may be regarded as substitutionable variables.[29]

Prices and norms. Prices correspond to normative standards. If the consumption at market prices runs counter to certain norms, these prices are often adjusted. This explains why alcohol is sold at an extremely high price, why drugs are prohibited, and why the theatre is subsidized. The market mechanism isn't infallible after all. The state intervenes because the price deviates from what should be exchanged in accordance with the obtaining norms.

These are not the only instances in which the price level is adjusted by norms. Social security is another. No reward without a productive achievement, that is how the market mechanism operates economically. Nevertheless the state takes it upon herself to support those who are destitute. She has taken over the support which in the distant past was given by relatives and neighbours on grounds of a normative obligation. A social norm of justice is expressed in money; the price one pays is the premium.

Market mechanism and social control. Finally a more comprehensive example from the domain of international trade. As known, the orthodox theory of the international division of labour is based on Ricardo's law of comparative advantages. This law purports the following. When the comparative costs of a commodity in one country differ from those in another, each of these countries has a comparative advantage, irrespec-

29. There is a song by a Dutch cabaret-artist, which runs as follows:
'Het was niet uit liefde, het was om je geld,
Je was niet mooi, maar welgesteld... etc.'
Translated: 'I didn't marry you for love, but for money,
You weren't exactly pretty, but then you were rich... etc.'
Even in marriage, conceived of as an exchange relationship, substitution of economic goods and social rewards occurs.

tive of their relative wealth or poverty. International trade will then increase the prosperity of these countries. Trade restraints are irrational. They imply keeping expensive production going and foregoing an obvious profit. So far so good.

The practice of everyday life, however, shows a quite different picture, hard to reconcile with the law of comparative costs. Eliminating trade restraints is a slow and difficult process. Many instances could be given, the disappointing results of the UNCTAD conferences is one. Evidently the international division of labour is thwarted. Why? Several explanations could be offered; in this article stress is laid on those aspects which come into prominence as a result of the interdisciplinary approach.

If one conceives of the market mechanism as a form of social control a surprising insight emerges. Within a group or country certain norms and prices exist. They express the preferences of the individual members with respect to exchanged social rewards and economic goods. Any outsider wishing to join a group has to conform to the group norms if he is to take part in the exchange transactions. When in Rome do as the Romans do. The adopted rates of social exchange – the norms – are protected from the world outside. Any outsider wishing to sell goods in a domestic market, consequently has to conform to the established prices. The allocation by the market mechanism is protected; tariffs forestall infringement. This behaviour is intelligible as a form of social control. We are 'we' and foreigners are different. Protectionism and nationalism go hand in hand.

A similar insight is gained into the problems of European economic integration. The resistance to integration cannot be explained by purely economic arguments. The fact that normative standards and the institutional structures based on them differ from one country to another is far more important. The U.S.A. don't have problems like these. An American is 'at home' in every State, which indicates that social life is more or less the same everywhere. The trouble with Europe is that Europeans should first learn to regard one another as compatriots, before being able to realize a common medium of exchange – economically as well as sociologically.

Finally, the currency of a number of non-western countries is not accepted in international transactions. Meant are those countries excluded from the I.M.F. whose currency is not convertible. They are also the countries where social transactions take place according to norms completely different from ours, or where social exchange is unpredictable on account of unstable political structures. As a result international exchange is hampered by norm-uncertainty or, what amounts to the same thing, the currency of these countries is distrusted as a medium of exchange.

In the beginning of this paper neoclassical economics was criticized because it stimulates unwarranted confidence in the maximizing effect of the market mechanism. If one also takes sociological variables into account this confidence becomes less self-evident. By introducing social rewards, norms and social control we have gained some insight into the matter. To further elaborate our point of view it is necessary to have another look at Homans.

2.6. Power and status

Power is hardly touched upon in neoclassical economics. Abandoning the assumption of perfect competition will, at least at the level of macro-economics, give rise to immense problems. Macro-models and oligopolistic competition have proved to be incompatible so far. Consequently, economists dealing with the phenomenon of power – institutionalists, neomarxists – usually dispense with the neoclassical approach.

And yet it is feasible to introduce the phenomenon of power into neoclassical economics. The gap between market and power may be bridged by means of the exchange theory.

In Homans' view, not every individual has the same capacity to reward others. Depending upon the relative scarcity, these capacities are variously valued. One who happens to have the qualities on which the highest value is put, has more to offer than someone who doesn't. Thus inequality of people leads to differences in power.

> 'Differences in power are differences in the capacity to reward others (to punish others)... Power, then depends on an ability to provide rewards that are valuable because they are scarce'.[30]

With Homans, power and status amount to virtually the same.

30. G.C. Homans, *Fundamental Social Processes,* 1967, p. 54.

'The origin of differences in status is differences in power, and men are powerful when many want what they, the few, are able to supply or many fear what they, the few, are able to withhold'.[31]

Homans' theory of power may be regarded as a translation of Clark's theory of income distribution. One need only substitute income for power, and marginal productivity for capacity to reward.

As known, Clark explains the earnings of the productive factors from their marginal products. Depending on the income-acquiring capacities of the productive factors – the number and relative scarcity of the goods produced – the incomes earned diverge. Thus differences in income (Clark) and differences in power (Homans) are similarly explained. In both cases inequality of people is postulated. Both arguments will lead to the same conclusion if we substitute power for income.

Looked at in this way, Clark's theory contains an interesting paradox. At bottom his explanation of the income distribution is a pure market theory. Inequality of income nevertheless arises, corresponding to the relative scarcity of income-acquiring capacities. In economics the purchasing power of individuals may differ without the phenomenon of power being touched upon.

A similar paradox arises when the economic concept of consumer sovereignty is identified with an equal – or democratic – determination of the resource allocation.[32] This is not very realistic. In western states the top 10 percent determines about 30 percent of the allocation, the bottom 20 percent but 5 percent.

An interdisciplinary approach offers a more consistent view. When inequality exists exchange relations are power relations. Differences in capacity to reward others entail differences in power. By rewards Homans means not only the so-called primary rewards, but also the indirect or contrived rewards. Money fits into the latter category but in explaining power the distinction is relatively unimportant. To Homans money is just one means of power, by no means the only one. Relevant to the interdisciplinary conception is the additional function that money has acquired: besides having the economic functions, medium of exchange and unit of account, money is also a source of power. Differences in income are differences in power.

31. *Ibid*, p. 59.
32. Myrdal speaks of 'the communist fiction' in this connection. G. Myrdal, *The Political Element in the Development of Economic Theory*, 1953.

2.7. The interdisciplinary conception II

The interdisciplinary conception is taking shape. The power phenomenon, too, fits in now. 'Market' and 'power' have proved to be quite compatible. This in contrast to neoclassical economics in which the market mechanism – perfect competition – is linked with the absence of power. Social exchange leads to differences in power if there is inequality among the exchanging subjects. Assuming equilibrium, the allocation of power reflects the relative scarcity of human qualities.

Just like prices (including incomes) and norms, power is established in the market. Power, too, is based on the preferences of exchanging individuals, concerning economic goods and social rewards. Knowledge is power, when the market mechanism assigns to intelligence a higher value than to skill. Money is power, when exchange transactions lead to an unequal income distribution.

The results so far may now be summarized as follows:

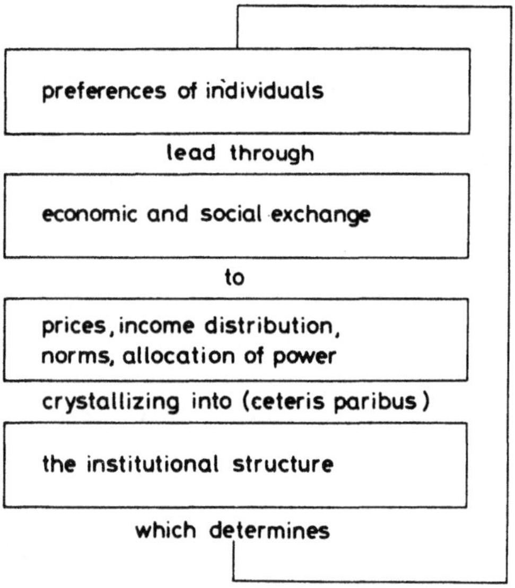

Conflict and change. The neoclassical conception of society has been extended, so as to accommodate norms, social control, power and the institutional structure. Yet a significant aspect of social life has been left out so far: conflict. More about this now.

Within the interdisciplinary conception conflicts may be conceived of

OUTLINE OF THE INTERDISCIPLINARY CONCEPTION

	relative stable individual preferences	rapidly changing individual preferences
norms	norms arise from social exchange (interaction) and regulate it in turn; they reflect the relative scarcity of social rewards	the regulation of social exchange decreases
prices	prices arise from economic exchange and regulate it in turn; they reflect the relative scarcity of economic goods and services	the regulation of economic exchange (by the market) decreases
social control	social control maintains stability; conformism yields maximum satisfaction of wants	social control is diminishing; generally accepted norms are rejected
market-mechanism	the market mechanism maintains stability; perfect competition yields (Pareto) optimality	the market mechanism is distorted; 'market-made' prices are rejected (monopolistic marketforms)
allocation of power	the allocation of power is established in the market and corresponds to the individual capacities to reward	the institutionalized allocation of power is challenged; exercise of power is experienced as coercion; adjustment is resisted by vested interests
income distribution	the income distribution is established in the market and corresponds to the individual contributions to production (marginal productivity)	the income distribution is challenged; differences in income are regarded as unjust; equalization is resisted by passing on the risen wage-costs to the consumer

as arising from changes in individual preferences. For convenience' sake we assume these changes to be caused by exogenous factors.[33] When the preferences of individuals, which in the past have led to prices, norms, etc. and which have been perpetuated by institutionalization, are altered, the relative scarcity of economic goods and social rewards is altered likewise. Norms and prices change. So should the power- and income distribution. The institutional structure is challenged; it no longer corresponds to what is expressed by actual exchange relations. Those

33. This is not strictly necessary; Blau, for instance, holds that the origin of conflicts is endogenous to the process of exchange. See the final section.

who are threatened with a diminution of their position will – as a result of an utilitarianistic orientation – resist change. 'Vested interests' have the institutional structure on their side, the latter being the substratum of the preferences in the original situation. Power, however, is no longer legitimated, and will be experienced as coercion. Likewise, the income distribution is experienced as unjust. Thus conflicts arise.[34]

It is important to notice in this respect that differences in power and income in themselves need not result in conflicts. Conflicts are first and foremost linked up with change, not with inequality. In primitive cultures, for instance, exchange relations often run along the same line for hundreds of years. The social structure is more or less stable. Differences in power, however, do occur. They have prevailed because they are legitimated by internalized norms.

What matters is whether inequality is experienced as norm(al). If so, conflicts will be exceptional. The casts system in India, the hierarchy in the Roman Catholic Church and the schoolmaster in front of his class, manage to survive, provided that the norms supporting these institutions are accepted. Changes are brought about by those who experience the status quo as unjust. In this respect the missionary and the revolutionist have much in common. Both resist the status quo, both want change. The professed religion or ideology is incompatible with the prevailing norms.

In the introduction to this paper several limitations of neoclassical economics were mentioned: the institutional structure is considered as a datum, power and conflict remain concealed, social change and its bearing on economic variables is abstracted from. The interdisciplinary conception now includes these aspects.

Cost-push inflation as illustration. A current and persistent problem in economic life is inflation. Particularly in the last decade the rate of inflation has accelerated alarmingly. So far no means have been found to reverse this trend. Both keynesian and monetary policy are relatively powerless. Simultaneously a considerable unemployment has developed, restricting the ways in which inflation might be fought.

The chief malefactor in the upswing of the price level in the 1970's is known as cost-push inflation. The difficulty with this relatively new kind

34. Alternative readings are possible. Another cause of conflicts is when those in authority create a social order which doesn't correspond to the obtaining norms. After a coup d'état, for instance, we often see that violent oppression is resorted to.

of inflation is that it behaves more or less autonomously. Presumably other forces are at work from those referred to in economic models, as f.e. is suggested by J. Zijlstra, the President of 'De Nederlandsche Bank':

> 'The fact that there is no reason why the inflationary process should reverse in the future is what's most alarming about the whole situation. The crux of the matter is that the power of certain groups to push up wages and prices has become greater than that of the governments and central banks to restrain them'.

A similar trend is noticed by Zijlstra's colleague, the Governor of the Bank of England:

> '... a fundamental change in attitudes has been occuring, both internationally and, perhaps even more strikingly, within most of our countries. There has, I think, been some erosion of the former general acceptance that a nation or group of individuals stood to gain most in the long run from adhering to a broad framework or rules. In place of this attitude, groups possessing potential monopoly or near-monopoly power – hitherto only latent – seem increasingly disposed to exercise their power, more or less in disregard of others, in attempts to change the distribution of income in their favour'.

Notably, both diagnoses of current inflation are stated in non-economic terms. 'The power of certain groups has increased too much', 'attitudes have fundamentally changed', 'groups no longer adhere to a broad framework of rules'.

The same applies to Zijlstra's therapy. To tip the balance of power he wants 'to influence public opinion – not half-heartedly, but vigorously and continually – in such a way that it will favour anti-inflationary policy'. Public opinion is called in to exorcise the festering evil. This may sound realistic, yet it is quite uneconomic. The remedies for inflation furnished by economic models are many and varied, but public opinion as an instrumental variable is not one of them.

From the interdisciplinary point of view cost-push inflation may be conceived of as the economic component of the process of rapid social change, so characteristic of western societies. Sociologically speaking, in times of rapid social change the obtaining norms lose their regulating functions, without new norms having sufficiently developed to give much support. Social exchange is de-regulated. Social control diminishes; the exercise of power is no longer legitimated by internalized norms and will be experienced as coercion. The adjustment of the institutional structure is resisted by vested interests. Thus conflicts arise.

However, if prices and norms, the market mechanism and social control, the income distribution and the allocation of power, are conceived of as similar phenomena, cost-push inflation appears to be inherent in the same process. Not only social exchange is disrupted, but also economic exchange. The market mechanism is distorted; in the markets of both final products and productive factors competition is restricted. In particular in the market of productive factors market control involves conflicts as everyone attempts to change the distribution of income in his favour. Equalization is resisted by passing on the risen wage-costs to the consumer. It is thus that inflation – or at least the cost-push variant of inflation – is caused.

2.8. Evaluation

What have we achieved? A rehabilitation of neoclassical economics? Yes and no. No, because its essence – a non-sociological equilibrium theory – has been discarded. Yes, because the interdisciplinary conception is in fact no more than a sociological extension of neoclassical economics. The homo economicus has come alive. Norms and social control, power and conflict have now been incorporated. Sociological insights may be applied to elucidate economic problems.

The value of the interdisciplinary approach may also be seen as follows. The neoclassical conception is limited to economic goods and services. Social life is considered irrelevant to the course of economic processes. When applied to stable societies this abstraction need not lead to difficulties. The market mechanism maintains stability, not because changes take place without causing conflicts, but because relatively stable individual preferences require little adjustment.

In our rapidly changing western societies things are different. Everywhere the status quo is being challenged. Ubiquitous conflicts (between employers and employees, between governors and governed, etc.) evidently co-determine the course of economic processes. Sociological variables should then be included, if economic problems are to be adequately analyzed. Neoclassical economics hasn't got the equipment, the interdisciplinary conception has.

It is precisely in times of rapid social change that the scope of neoclassical economics proves to be too narrow. And it is precisely then that equilibrium is replaced by disequilibrium, that legitimated exercise of power is replaced by coercion and conflict, that the institutional structure is continually challenged. The 'ceteris' which do not remain 'paribus' call for an extension of the neoclassical conception.

Yet, the interdisciplinary conception is open to criticism. What Deutsch and Kraus say about Homans applies here too:

> 'Homans' theory implies that there is a common currency or a simple dimension to which the value of different experiences ('getting a B on an exam', 'being kissed by one's sweetheart', 'hearing a Beethoven quartet', 'being served a cold beer') can be co-ordinated so that the value of a 'unit' of one such activity received can be compared with the value of another unit. If there is a common currency of 'value', it has not yet been identified'.[37]

This criticism is less serious than it seems. In fact neither exchange theory nor economics *imply* that there is a common currency of value. The only one to compare *values* is the individual actor himself. His subjective considerations, determining the choices he makes, are nobody's business but his own. Both neoclassical economics and exchange theory only *assume* that his actual behaviour coincides with the maximum attainable satisfaction. Strickly speaking, there is no need for a common currency of value, enabling either a personal or an interpersonal comparison of satisfactions.

Assuming maximizing behaviour, nevertheless, has other risks. Any behaviour may be interpreted as such; the concept becomes a tautology. This same objection is often raised against the 'homo economicus', and it remains to be seen whether this objection is valid. Science is impossible without some kind of 'a priori'; establishing facts is always preceded by some kind of conception of reality. A priori conceptions defy falsification; they resemble creeds more than anything else. The criterion by which to judge them is whether falsifiable hypotheses can be deduced, in order to explain why things happen the way they do. As far as this is concerned the interdisciplinary conception has, in principle, the same possibilities as neoclassical economics.

Another possible critcism of the interdisciplinary conception is its incompleteness. In particular little attention has been paid to the phenomenon of social change and its corollary conflict. Here, sociology and institutional economics furnish clues for a more detailed examination. Another, perhaps more obvious way to extend our knowledge might

37. M. Deutsch and R. Kraus, *Theories in Social Psychology*, New York, 1965, pp. 114-115.

be the exchange theory of Peter M. Blau, in whose work equilibrium figures far less than in that of Homans:

'Arguments about equilibrium... ignore the important point that the forces sustaining equilibrium on one level of social life constitute disequilibrating forces on other levels... The principle suggested is that balanced social states depend on imbalances in other social states: forces that restore equilibrium in one respect do so by creating disequilibrium in others'.[38]

In Blau's conception of social exchange the origin of disequilibria is attributed to endogenous causes. There is no harmony without conflict. This view opens interesting perspectives for a further extension of the interdisciplinary conception.

38. Peter M. Blau, *Exchange and Power in Social life,* 1964, p. 12.

3. Institutional versus orthodox economics and the interdisciplinary approach

Allan G. Gruchy

3.1. Economics and the problem of relevancy

Since the end of the Second World War there has developed a growing dissatisfaction with the traditional separation of the social sciences as represented by the traditional departmental organization of our university activities.[1] Much of this dissatisfaction appears to have arisen as a consequence of the kinds of problems that have come to the attention of social scientists in recent decades, problems for whose analysis the scientific paradigm of the orthodox economists has not been found particularly useful. These problems include the conflicts over the selection of national goals and priorities, the social costs of economic growth, the plight of the less developed countries, the deterioration of the natural environment, the decline of social amenities and the need for urban renewal, the population explosion in the underdeveloped countries, and racial and sexual discrimination. Even those nations that enjoy what is described as affluence are beginning to question the goal of an ever-rising standard of living, and a great deal is heard these days of the goals of zero economic and zero population growth.[2] The handling of these pressing problems has emphasized the limited scopes of the individual social sciences, and has also called attention to the need for an interdisciplinary approach in dealing with these problems.

How economists will attempt to adjust or amend their science in order

1. E.H. Phelps Brown, 'The Underdevelopment of Economics', Presidential Address to the Royal Economic Society, July 8, 1971, and G.D.N. Worswick, 'Is Progress in Economic Science Possible?', Presidential Address to Section F of the British Association for the Advancement of Science, Sept. 2, 1971. Both addresses were published in *Economic Journal,* Vol. 82, March, 1972. For a similar view from an American source see Wassily Leontief, 'Theoretical Assumptions and Nonobserved Facts', *American Economic Review,* Vol. LXI, March, 1971, pp. 1-7.
2. Mancur Olson and Hans H. Landsberg (Eds.), *The No-Growth Society,* New York: W.W. Norton, 1972.

to make it a more effective instrument for treating present-day economic and social problems will be influenced to a large extent by their views on the nature and scope of economics. As we shall see, standard economists who reduce economics to the science of choosing, and who have a narrow view of the scope of economics, will be prone to leave the received economics intact or unaltered in any program for making this economics more relevant to the pressing issues of the second half of the twentieth century. If large, complicated problems call for more than standard economic analysis, then the matter can be taken care of in the opinion of orthodox economists by opening the door to the contributions of the other social sciences in ways that do not call for any major alteration in the scope of what Kenneth E. Boulding refers to as 'pure economics'. This has been done recently, for example, in the case of the construction of social indicators which relate to the social aspects of human well-being, and which are added by orthodox economists to their economic indicators with the aim of providing a better measure of human welfare. No matter how many social indicators are added to the economic indicators, the scope of the received or orthodox economics remains intact.

Another way orthodox economists have of leaving the corpus of their pure economics intact, and of thus preserving the traditional view of the scope of economics while they take account of non-economic data, is to go entirely beyond the received or conventional economics and to develop what Boulding has called a 'unified or general social science'.[3] This queen of the social sciences is then called upon to deal with such problems as economic growth in a world of finite resources, the deterioration of the natural and social environments, the population explosion, and the plight of the less developed countries. Whatever route orthodox economists follow in their efforts to move beyond the limitations of their market economics, they see to it that this economics is left intact.

While the institutionalists agree that much good work has been done by orthodox economists in recent years by moving into the area of extra-market or public sector economics and in making use of the contributions of the other social sciences, the institutionalists believe that economists would be better prepared to cooperate with other social

3. Kenneth E. Boulding, *Beyond Economics,* Ann Arbor: University of Michigan Press, 1968, p.v.

scientists in dealing with major human problems, if they were to start off with a broader view of the nature and scope of economics. The broad view of the nature and scope of economics that the institutionalists have leads them to analyze many problems of great interest to other social scientists. These problems include the impact of technological change on the structure and functioning of the social system, the power relations among various interest groups, the determination of national goals and priorities, the logic of industrialization, the logic of economic and social reform, and the direction in which the economic and social systems are moving. The analysis of these problems requires going beyond the limited 'market economics' of the orthodox economists, and developing a broader 'systems economics' that takes the economic system to be an evolving process. From the viewpoint of systems economics the economic system in the advanced industrial economies is seen to be in a process of transition from an era in which technological change was slow and limited to an era in which it is very rapid and explosive in nature. In the case of the United States the transition is from regulated welfare capitalism to some form of planned organizational or technological capitalism.

In the opinion of the institutionalists the narrow scope of received economics and the efforts of orthodox economists to preserve its limited scope even in the face of interdisciplinary studies are obstacles to making this economics more relevant to the handling of major economic and social problems, and to making it a more effective partner in various interdisciplinary programs. What limits the relevance of orthodox economists to the economic and social issues of the last quarter of the twentieth century is their scientific paradigm or overall analytical construct in the light of which they analyze the modern industrial system. This received paradigm is, in the opinion of the institutionalists, an inadequate device for grasping the nature of advanced industrial economies. It is much too static and much too restricted in nature to enable us to comprehend economic and social reality fully. The institutionalists' scientific paradigm is both dynamic and comprehensive, and is, in the opinion of Gunnar Myrdal and other institutionalists, a more satisfactory analytical construct for understanding the nature of economic and social reality.

3.2. The relevance of orthodox economics

While orthodox economists widely agree that there is a need to go beyond the received economics in dealing with many human problems, they take different approaches towards this issue of how their economics should be made more relevant. One group of orthodox economists has a static, short-run approach to this problem of relevancy, while the other group has a dynamic, long-run approach to the same problem. The first group is especially concerned with the extra-market problems that arise in the public sector, where public or collective goods are produced and consumed outside the private market system. These orthodox economists find a need to apply a sociological perspective to current activities in the public sector, because in this sector budgetary funds are spent on such non-marketable collective goods as education, public health, defense, law and order, and aid to the arts and sciences. In the United States recent attempts by the Department of Health, Education, and Welfare to chart the nation's social progress by developing a regular system of social reporting with the aid of social indicators have called attention to the need to supplement the economic indicators of the Council of Economic Advisers.[4] The orthodox economists with the static, short-run approach propose to enlist the aid of sociologists, political scientists, anthropologists, and psychologists in developing a multidisciplinary approach to the problem of improving social well-being. This would be achieved by adding to the Council of Economic Advisers' 'traditional and proper occupation with "macroeconomics" questions – the problems of recession and inflation, or the fluctuations of the market sector as a whole... "social" problems that have not been given much attention in the [annual] Economic Report [of the Council]'.[5] Orthodox economists would in this manner make economics more relevant by extending decision making from private market economics to public sector economics, where the analysis would include both economic and non-economic data.

The second group of orthodox economists would improve the relevancy of their received economics by going beyond static market and

4. U.S. Department of Health, Education, and Welfare, *Toward a Social Report*, Washington, D.C.: U.S. Government Printing Office, 1969.

5. Mancur Olson, Jr., 'The Relationship between Economics and the Other Social Sciences: The Province of a "Social Report",' in Seymour Martin Lipset (Ed.), *Politics and the Social Sciences*, New York: Oxford University Press, 1969, p. 160.

public sector economics to an evolutionary, overall or general social science, which would be quite unlike any of the traditional social science disciplines. A well-known exponent of this universalistic approach is Kenneth E. Boulding who has defended both 'the purity of economics as a discipline and the necessity for moving forward in a more general social science'.[6] Boulding approves of the contributions of the static, short-run orthodox economists, but he feels a need to go beyond them and to introduce a dynamic element into social science analysis. He does this by taking society, that is to say the total social system, to be an evolving process which has undergone two major transitions. The first transition was from the pre-civilized society, before cities had become established, to the current civilized or urban society. The next transition, if it occurs, will be from the civilized society to the post-civilized society. In the current century research and development have become greatly institutionalized, and there has been a large increase in the rate of change of both knowledge and technology. As a result of scientific advance and technological change we are, according to Boulding's interpretation, in a 'great transition' which may take us from the civilized society to the post-civilized society.[7] In the latter society the integrative forces would be sufficiently strong to establish a society in which there would be peace, abundance, and freedom. The final outcome of a 'genuinely developmental integrative society' is possible, but not inevitable.[8] As Boulding sees it, war, the population explosion, and ecological disaster may deny our arriving at the post-civilized society.

The dynamic factor in Boulding's concept of the evolutionary society is human knowledge and the science and technology to which it gives rise. He explains that 'The great transitions in the state of mankind... may be identified primarily with changes in the state of human knowledge, involving therefore a learning process'.[9] Other factors such as purely physical events, wars, and political developments may result in profound changes in man's culture, but the primary factor in social change remains 'human learning and the processes by which knowledge is acquired'. Changes in technology produce changes in social and

6. *Beyond Economics*, p. v.
7. For an elaboration of Boulding's thesis of the 'great transition' see his analysis in *The Meaning of the Twentieth Century*, New York: Harper and Row, 1964.
8. Kenneth E. Boulding, *A Primer on Social Dynamics, History as Dialectics and Development*, New York: The Free Press, 1970, p. 110.
9. *The Meaning of the Twentieth Century*, p. 174.

economic institutions, and in turn changes in these institutions produce changes in technology. Changes in technology and institutions are interrelated and affect each other in a circular way. However, according to Boulding's interpretation, there is nothing inevitable or deterministic about technological change. He makes no use of the concept of a logic of technological development as the result of which industrial economies tend to pass through a common pattern of economic development. As Boulding puts it, 'in the case of knowledge, and, one might even add, technology, prediction of the future is impossible'.[10] Unlike the institutionalists, Boulding does not take technological change to be an imperative that channels the course of industrial development, and in effect imposes something of a common pattern on industrialized economies.

Boulding has an oversimplified view of the world in which all countries are divided into the democratic countries of the West and the socialist or communist countries of the East. In his view, the western nations have relied primarily on the unplanned market mechanism in their efforts to achieve economic development, whereas the eastern nations have relied mainly on centralized planning for the same purpose. Boulding sees deficiencies in both methods of fostering economic development, and he concludes that the proper goal is 'the optimum mix of the market and budget [or planning] mechanism'.[11] Nothing is said by Boulding about the democratically planned economies of Sweden, Norway, The Netherlands, and France that lie between the unplanned capitalist economies of the West and the highly centralized and authoritarian economies of the East. In Boulding's objective of a 'guided market economy' the emphasis is on the functioning of the private market mechanism, and not on the guidance that would be provided by the government.

Boulding and orthodox economists, who have widened the area of their scientific interests in recent decades, still fail to take adequate account of many of the dynamic factors in economic and social life that are of interest to the institutionalists. What these orthodox economists do is to introduce into their science what is described by Warren J. Samuels as his 'market-plus framework interpretation'.[12] In utilizing this

10. Kenneth E. Boulding, *The Impact of the Social Sciences,* New Brunswick, N.J.: Rutgers University Press, 1966, p. 21.

11. *The Meaning of the Twentieth Century,* p. 174.

12. For an analysis of this market-plus framework interpretation see Warren J. Samuels, *The Classical Theory of Economic Policy,* New York: World Publishing Co., 1966, pp. 1-20

analytical framework these orthodox economists push their analyses out from their market economics, that is to say, they inquire into the legal, social, and political systems that surround the market system. When they move beyond the market system, the economists who take this system as their point of departure are prone to underestimate the significance of the impact of technological change on the structure and functioning of the economic system. They also have little to say about the logic of the process of industrialization that influences the shape of the evolving industrial system. In addition, these orthodox economists pay little attention to the logic of economic reform that points the evolving industrial system in the direction of some form of planned collective action. The market-plus framework analysis has severe limitations as a method of making orthodox economics more relevant to twentieth-century economic and social issues, limitations which show up in the work of Boulding, Samuelson, Robbins, and others who adhere to a conventional view of the nature and scope of 'pure economics'.

3.3. The relevance of institutional economics

In their efforts to make their economics relevant to the economic and social issues of the fourth quarter of the twentieth century the institutionalists are not faced with the same problem that is presented to orthodox economists because of the narrow scope of the latter economists' received economics. This is the case because the institutionalists have a view of economics that assigns to it a broad scope.[13] Their

and 237-288. Samuels borrows his market-plus framework interpretation from the orthodox, anti-institutionalist Lionel Robbins, who presented his views along this line in *The Theory of Economic Policy in English Classical Political Economy* (1952). Robbins' review of English classical political economy is an effort to show that the classical economists from David Hume to John Stuart Mill had a broader view of economics than is usually attributed to them by their critics. Both Samuels and Robbins, who take the market system as their point of departure in these volumes, do not have the technological interpretation of the process of industrialization of the mainstream institutionalists from Veblen on, and also do not make use of the concepts of the logic of industrialization and the logic of economic reform employed by these institutionalists. Robbins is highly critical of the institutionalists, while Samuels, who describes Robbins' approach to economics as 'seminal' (*The Classical Theory of Economic Policy*, p. 5), claims to be an institutionalist, but remains outside the mainstream of institutionalism as found in the work of Veblen, Clark, Mitchell, Colm, Galbraith, and Myrdal.

13. The views of the pre-1939 and the post-1939 institutionalists on the nature and scope of economics are presented in Allan G. Gruchy, *Modern Economic Thought, The American*

explanation of the economic system involves not only a study of the internal operations of this system, but also studies of the impact of the larger cultural system on the economic system and of the impact of the economic system on the larger cultural system. The approach to economics developed by the institutionalists has led them to substitute a 'systems economics' for the narrow 'market economics' of the orthodox economists. The institutionalists have an interest in explaining the nature of the market system, but their explanation of the market system is a part of their broader explanation of the functioning of the total industrial system. They shift attention away from the theory of the market mechanism to a theory of the whole economic system, which in the United States becomes a theory of mature capitalism or of a mature mixed economy. In developing their theory of the advanced industrial economy the institutionalists go beyond the narrow limits set for economics by orthodox economists. Almost 40 years ago John Maurice Clark said, in discussing the boundaries of economics, that 'Unless they have been finally and authoritatively established in some writing which has escaped my notice, I feel free to contend that it is less important to keep inside any traditional limits than to follow our natural questionings wherever they may lead, and do whatever work we are specially fitted for and find undone'.[14] Twenty years later Gunnar Myrdal also abandoned the conventional boundaries of the received economics when analyzing the long-term developmental trends of the mature and less developed economies. In his economic analysis Myrdal does away with the distinction between 'non-economic' and 'economic' factors, and emphasizes instead what are 'relevant' and 'irrelevant' factors, or what are 'more relevant' and 'less relevant' factors.[15] Galbraith likewise observes that 'The boundaries of a subject matter [like economics] are conventional and artificial; none should use them as an excuse for excluding the important... Accordingly, in the later chapters I turn to the effects of economic change on social and political behavior, and to remedy and reform'.[16]

Contribution, New York: Prentice-Hall, 1947, and *Contemporary Economic Thought, The Contributions of Neo-Institutional Economics,* Clifton, N.J.: Augustus M. Kelley, 1972.

14. John M. Clark, 'Toward a Concept of Social Value', in *Preface to Social Economics,* New York: Farrar and Rinehart, 1936, p. 65.

15. Gunnar Myrdal, *Rich Lands and Poor, The Road to World Prosperity,* New York: Harper and Brothers, 1957, p. 10.

16. John Kenneth Galbraith, *The New Industrial State,* Boston: Houghton Mifflin, 1967, p. 7.

Unlike the orthodox economists who would deal with the problems of a rapidly changing world by leaving pure economics intact, and by enlisting the aid of other social scientists in the effort to deal with these problems in an interdisciplinary way, the instititutionalists alter the contents of their economics as circumstances warrant. Since their economics already has a very broad scope, what is at issue is not their views on the proper scope of economics but what kinds of data this scope should include. The pre-1939 institutionalists such as Veblen, Clark, and Mitchell had the same views on the proper scope of economics as do the post-1939 institutionalists such as Galbraith, Ayres, Colm, and Myrdal. What have changed over the years since 1900 have been the kinds of problems that the institutionalists have brought within the scope of their science. Veblen's economics dealt with the problems associated with the rise of large-scale or monopoly capitalism in the years 1890-1925. The institutional economics of Mitchell, Clark, and Commons who came after Veblen was greatly influenced by the decline of laissez-faire capitalism and the rise of welfare capitalism in the 1930s. The economics of the post-1939 neo-institutionalists has been focused on the shift from welfare capitalism to guided capitalism, and on the problems associated with the call for zero economic and zero population growth in a world of finite natural resources. This is not to say that the neo-institutionalists do not cooperate with other social scientists where an interdisciplinary approach is useful. On the contrary, they welcome joint consultation and joint action among social scientists. It is their position, however, that their systems economics has much to contribute to multidisciplinary work in the area of the social sciences that goes beyond the contributions of the private-public sector economics of the orthodox economists. This is the case, in the opinion of the institutionalists, because their evolutionary scientific paradigm is much broader in scope than is the static paradigm of the orthodox economists.[17]

17. A comparison of these two economic paradigms is presented in Allan G. Gruchy, 'The Neo-institutionalist Paradigm and the Limitations of Keynesian Economics', *Eastern Economic Journal*, (forthcoming), 1975. See also Allan G. Gruchy, 'The Scientific Paradigm of the Institutionalists', (mimeo), a paper delivered at the Colorado State University, Fort Collins, Colorado, April 9, 1976.

3.4. The institutionalists' three-sector model of the economy

According to the interpretation of the institutionalists the evolving western industrial economy has now reached the stage of the three-sector or triplistic economy. In explaining this economy the institutionalists have developed a theoretical model in which the government, the private oligopolistic, and the private competitive sectors interact with one another. The private oligopolistic sector includes the large financial and industrial enterprises and the large trade unions. The private competitive sector takes in the small-scale business firms, the farms, and the service trades, while the government sector is made up of various administrative agencies and public enterprises. The large-scale oligopolistic sector is the progressive sector where most of the economic growth, research and development, and innovation takes place. This sector has a high per capita share of the national income and possesses very considerable economic power. In the unregulated capitalist economy the oligopolistic sector exploits the competitive sector in which business firms have little market power, little technological advance and economic growth occur, per capita income is low, and labor is frequently poorly organized. Although the oligopolistic sector is more advanced than the competitive sector, the former sector is the source of great economic instability, and also suffers from strong inflationary pressures. When a recession occurs the oligopolistic sector contracts and reduces investment, production, and employment, whereas in the competitive sector the small business firms, farms, and service trades continue to operate as long as they can, thus maintaining considerable employment and production even in recessions.

The government sector in the triplistic industrial economy, besides providing an important part of the gross national product, also acts in a mediating or reconciling manner in relation to the two private sectors. The government sector provides national economic guidance by setting up regulatory bodies, by intervening at strategic points in the economy, and in some cases adopting national planning programs. This national guidance is particularly concerned with the determination of national goals and priorities and the construction of an effective incomes policy. In the absence of adequate national guidance the oligopolistic sector exploits the competitive sector by undermining the latter sector's efficiency and good performance with the aid of administered prices and wages and other noncompetitive devices.

The institutionalists analyze the modern industrial economy on three different levels: the short-run, the medium-term, and the long-range levels. Like other economists the institutionalists are very much interested in current or short-run economic activities as they relate to the ups and downs of the economic system. They are also concerned with medium-term (four or five year) economic developments which include corporate investment plans, research and development, provisions for manpower, and regional expansion. Finally, the institutionalists are very much interested in long-range economic activities over 15 to 20 year periods in which scientific advances and technological changes occur, long-term investment commitments are made, changes in educational and manpower requirements are considered, and significant changes in industrial structure are introduced. These long-term economic and social developments work themselves out slowly and irregularly. Their influence or impact may be held back for a time, as water is impounded by a dam, only to burst forth with very disturbing results after years of accumulation. The scientific advances and technological changes of the past few decades now appear to be breaking through the high wall of antiquated economic doctrines and practices to create a demand for an economy that can more effectively serve the national interest than does the unplanned mixed economy now found in the United States, the United Kingdom, and some other industrialized West European countries.

Currently the industrial economies of Western Europe and the United States are seen by the institutionalists to be in an era of transition from the regulated mixed economy to the planned mixed economy. In this situation a heavy burden falls on the government sector to provide guidance for the nation's economy in both its domestic and external affairs. The western industrial economies are not all at the same stage in their evolutionary development. Some like the United States have not yet gotten beyond regulation and intervention. In some planning has made very little progress as in the United Kingdom and Italy, but in France, The Netherlands, Norway, and Sweden national planning became well established after 1945, as these countries moved from uncoordinated intervention to what Gunnar Myrdal has described as coordinated intervention or national planning.[18] What the western

18. Gunnar Myrdal, *Beyond The Welfare State*, New Haven: Yale University Press, 1960, p. 63.

industrial economies now seek is a managed or programmed equilibrium in which the activities of their three sectors would be harmoniously interrelated.

3.5. Institutional economics and the concept of the evolving economic process

One of the most common criticisms of the received economics is that it does not analyze the economic system as an evolving process. This criticism usually emphasizes the failure of orthodox economics of both the Marshallian and Keynesian types to analyze the long-run changes in the structure and functioning of the economic system. The institutionalists, who have specialized in the application of the 'long view' to economic analysis, have stressed the evolutionary aspects of economic activities. Veblen traced economic development from the Stone Age up to the 'finance' or 'monopoly' capitalism of the 1920s, but his primary concern was with the period from 1875 to 1925 when small-scale, competitive capitalism was converted into large-scale, monopoly capitalism. Mitchell and Clark in the United States and Tawney and Cole in England analyzed the period 1910-1939 during which large-scale, laissez-faire capitalism reached its zenith and was followed by the welfare capitalism of the 1930s. Colm, Galbraith, and Myrdal have applied their long-view, evolutionary analysis to the period 1930-1970 during which the mixed economy of the West has moved from the relatively uncoordinated interventionism of the 1930s and 1940s to the coordinated interventionism or planning of the 1950s and 1960s.

The institutionalists have different views from those of Boulding and other orthodox economists with regard to the causes of economic and social change, and with regard to how the socio-economic process develops. With respect to the question of the causes of economic and social change the institutionalists assign a more significant role to technological change as the cause of social and economic change than do orthodox economists. They have a middle position between those who may be called technological determinists, such as Marx and Veblen are alleged to be, and those who wish to avoid being classed as technological determinists and so do not make much out of technological change as a factor leading to economic and social change. It is the institutionalists' position that technology is an imperative or causal factor of great significance in economic and social development. Technology and the science that it draws upon are the result of a long cumulative process in which they come to have an existence of their own. Technology as an imperative is in some ways independent of the behavior of individuals.[19] Although man can influence the course of scientific and technological advance, this advance becomes a powerful force in cultural affairs that influences the shape of economic and social development in ways that are at times beyond human control.

While technological change is, according to Myrdal and other institutionalists, the mainspring of economic and social development, other political, social, and physical factors are recognized as having some influence upon the course of economic and social development. Galbraith asserts that technology, organization, and ideology have an influence on the pattern of industrial development, but ideology plays a minor role. Technological change results in the setting up of large-scale industrial and political organizations, which in turn stimulate further technological change by funding research and development. This research and development then leads to further scientific and technological advance. In this circular cumulative causation a primary force such as technological change leads to a secondary factor in the form of more complex large-scale economic and political organizations, which later reinforce the primary force of technological change. While a number of factors contribute to economic and social development, technological change remains the outstanding developmental imperative or compulsion in the opinion of the institutionalists.

The second point with regard to technological change that separates the institutionalists from orthodox economists calls attention to the concept of the logic of economic development. There are three ways of viewing the course of economic development. The first way is to say that there are laws which govern the course of this development. Marx's dynamics of capitalist development was based on inevitable trends or contradictions that are regarded by present-day Soviet economists as laws of development. These Marxian laws of motion that are applied to economic development bear no resemblance to the laws of pure economics that were developed in the nineteenth century. Most western

19. As Galbraith expresses it, 'In examining the intricate complex of economic change, technology, having an initiative of its own, is the logical point at which to break in'. See *The New Industrial State*, p. 20.

economists do not find the concept of economic law as applied to economic development to be a useful concept, since the data of economic development support few generalizations of a universal nature.

The second way to view the course of economic development is to assume that there is no pattern or order in the course of this development. According to this view economic development is a haphazard, directionless process which may be described but which is not the source of any laws or principles of development. Economic historians, who limit themselves to the description of the course of economic development, adopt the position that this development is without any predictable shape or pattern, and so is essentially a blind process.

The third position, which is that of the institutionalists, involves viewing the economic system as an evolving process which gives expression to an inherent logic of development. According to this interpretation economic, social, and political processes 'come into existence, and grow, and change by a logic of their own'.[20] The concept of the logic of economic development is derived from the concept of the logic of cultural development, which states that men in similar environmental circumstances will tend to develop common or similar cultural patterns. In other words, there is a logic of circumstances which gives shape or pattern to cultural development. Similarly, in the opinion of the institutionalists, the prevailing circumstances of the industrialized countries, prominent among which is the state of science and technology, give rise to certain common features of industrial development. The logic of industrial development indicates in a broad kind of way the course that the advanced industrialized countries will probably follow in their evolution. While the world's industrialized nations exhibit considerable economic, social, and political diversity, at the same time they reveal considerable industrial uniformity, which arises out of the uniformity of the basic technology shared by all industrialized countries. The imperatives of industrialism lead to an urbanized society, a large role for the government, large-scale industrial organization and the problem of the managers and the managed, an educational system attuned to the needs of industry, and an open society with much occupational mobility. As Clark Kerr has expressed it, 'Industrialism has as its greatest imperative the conquest of the old by the new, and it is compelling

20. C.E. Ayres, *The Industrial Economy,* Boston: Houghton Mifflin, 1952, p. 40.

mankind to march through history at an ever faster rate. But it sets only the general direction of this march. It does not... set the specific route of the march or the exact pace to be followed'.[21]

3.6. Institutionalism and the logic of reform

Divergent views about the role of technology in economic and social development and about trends or tendencies in the economic and social process lead to divergent views concerning the probable shape of the future industrial society. This is a question of the direction in which the socio-economic process may be moving. While the institutionalists do not predict in any detailed way the next stage in the development of the advanced industrial economies, they do believe that it is possible to say something significant about the probable shape of the future industrial society. The institutionalists analyze this probable shape in terms of a logic of economic reform, which is an extension of their logic of industrial development.[22] This logic of economic reform points in the direction of what Daniel Bell describes as a post-industrial society in which economic activities will become increasingly collective in nature, and in which the government will have to reconcile the interests of major economic pressure groups. Such efforts will require a considerable degree of planning at both the national and international levels.

A number of industrialized nations already have well developed national planning programs in operation as one can observe in Sweden, Norway, The Netherlands, Belgium, and France. In West Germany where there is close cooperation between the central and state governments, business, the large banks, and the major trade unions in the construction and execution of economic policies, there is apparently no need for any formal planning of the French or Scandinavian type. In the United Kingdom it was the Conservative Government that established the National Economic Development Council in 1962, and had this Council construct a six year national plan for the years 1963-1968. The British Labour Party has also advocated national planning, but it has not remained in office long enough to place this planning on a firm

21. Clark Kerr et al., *Industrialism and Industrial Man*, Cambridge, Mass.: Harvard University Press, 1960, p. 47.
22. This point is developed in *Modern Economic Thought, The American Contribution*, pp. 620-621.

organizational foundation. In the United States considerable coordination of economic policy has been achieved with the aid of the Council of Economic Advisers which was established in 1946. In some quarters it is felt that a greater effort should be made to place policy formulation in the United States on a longer term and more formal basis with the aid of a national economic planning board. Wassily Leontief has recently proposed that an Office of National Economic Planning be established in the United States to submit to the Congress intermediate five or six year and long-term 15 to 25 year plans, which would be designed to carry the nation towards its long-range objectives.[23] Leontief's proposal is along the line recommended by Galbraith who has said that for the United States 'the creation of the planning machinery, which the present structure of the economy makes imperative, is the next major task in economic design'.[24] These planning proposals are but a continuation of the long line of planning proposals that began with Veblen in the early post World War I years, and that were later repeated but in different form by Clark, Mitchell, Tugwell, and Means.

Orthodox economists in the United States do not make use of the concept of a logic of economic reform. They do not anticipate any major alteration in the structure and functioning of the advanced industrial system, and have as their goal a policy that would lead to what they describe as 'workable competition'.[25] They call for a vigorous enforcement of the antitrust laws in order to reduce the monopolistic imperfections of the mature American economy. This vigorous enforcement of the antitrust laws would be supported by a public vigilance that would detect deviations from the norms of competitive enterprise. Other orthodox economists, who have a dynamic approach to the study of the mature mixed economy, see a need to go beyond vigorous enforcement of the antitrust laws, but not so far as to establish any formal national planning program. Like Boulding these orthodox economists would regulate, direct, or guide the market economy, but they would not plan its affairs in any formal way. They would seek to remove certain deficiencies in the modern industrial economy such as the lack of an

23. Wassily Leontief, 'What an Economic Planning Board Should Do', *Challenge*, Vol. 17, July/August, 1974, pp. 35-40 and *The New York Times*, March 15, 1974.
24. John Kenneth Galbraith, *Economics and the Public Purpose*, Boston: Houghton Mifflin, 1973, p. 319.
25. Prominent among the advocates of 'workable competition' is Paul A. Samuelson. His views on this matter are presented in *Economics*, Ninth Edition, New York: McGraw-Hill, 1973, pp. 528-529.

adequate supply of public goods, an inequitable distribution of income, inadequate provision for people who stand in need of tranfer incomes, and serious economic instability. All this would be done, however, without resort to any form of indicative democratic national planning such as is found in a number of West European countries. It is this lack of interest in national planning on the part of the orthodox economists that sets them off very distinctly from the institutionalists in the area of policy making and execution.

3.7. Institutional economics and macro-sociology

There are very close connections between institutional economics and the area of sociology described as 'macro-sociology'.[26] This sociology is concerned with the evolution of the social system, the factors leading to this evolution, and the direction in which the social system may be moving. Macro-sociologists, like the institutionalists, have a futuristic view of social science. They assert that one of the functions of social science is to indicate the probable nature of the next era of the emerging social system. Macro-sociologists as well as the institutionalists believe that there is a basic logic in the evolution of society, and that an analysis of this logic can reveal some of the features of the coming post-industrial society.

We may take as representative of the views of the macro-sociologists

26. Daniel Bell describes his type of sociology as 'macro-sociology'. A better description of it would be 'systems sociology' since his work is closer to the evolutionary economics of the institutionalists than to the static Keynesian 'macroeconomics', See Daniel Bell, *The Coming of Post-Industrial Society, A Venture in Social Forecasting,* New York: Basic Books, 1973, p. xii. Like many other sociologists who are interested in the relations between economics and sociology, Bell seems largely unaware of the contributions of the institutional school, and he assumes that 'economics' is essentially or mainly Keynesian economics. Neil J. Smelser, who is apparently even less acquainted with the contributions of Veblen, Clark, Mitchell, Ayres, Galbraith, and Myrdal than is Bell, takes Paul A. Samuelson to be the archetypal figure in the realm of economic thought. (See Neil J. Smelser, *The Sociology of Economic Life,* 1963, p. 23). Since the institutionalists do precisely what Smelser wants economic sociologists to do, namely, analyse 'the social setting in which economic life is embedded' (p. v) – something that Samuelson and other Keynesian do not do – one would have thought that Smelser would have analyzed the new well-documented contributions of the institutional economists in his 1963 study of the sociology of economic life. According to his later writings Smelser still takes Samuelson to be the prototypal economist. American sociology would make more progess in its relations with economics, if it was more aware of the limitations of Keynesian economics which is now the new orthodoxy in economics.

the views of Daniel Bell which have recently been presented in *The Coming of Post-Industrial Society*. Bell's analysis of the emerging post-industrial society starts with his scientific paradigm or analytical construct of this emerging society. This is a paradigm that cuts across many industrial countries including the United States, the Soviet Union, Western Europe, and Japan. The main features of Bell's scientific paradigm are a social structure that includes the economy and the technicians that direct it, the culture with its emphasis upon modernism and the expression of the individual self, and the polity or political system whose main function is to manage the social structure. The society of which the social structure, culture, and polity are basic parts is a knowledge or technological society in which goods production has been replaced in large part by service production, technicians have a key role as sources of innovation, and the new reality is the social world in which men live and encounter one another.

In Bell's scientific paradigm there is a deep conflict between the social structure dominated by the technical elites with bourgeois values, who are interested in rationality and efficiency, and the culture with its exponents of modernism and permissiveness in the news media and the arts. Bell observes a basic dichotomy between the technicians who emphasize production, provident behavior, industriousness, and self-control and the cultural leaders in literature and the arts whose anti-bourgeois values support a life style of personal freedom, extreme experiences, and sexual experimentation. This disjunction of culture and social structure has a psychological basis in what Bell describes as the 'duplex nature of man himself', which expresses itself as a conflict between self and society, or between man's aggressive personal drives and his search for order in life.[27]

When Bell turns to his analysis of the post-industrial society in action, he states that this society will become increasingly a communal society in which more attention will be paid to community welfare than has been the case up to now. The government will have the function of acting as an arbiter among competing group interests with the aim of reducing groupal conflict. The new emphasis will be on 'sociologizing' and not on 'economizing'. Special efforts will be made to determine society's needs

27. *Ibid.*, p. 488. See also Daniel Bell, 'The Cultural Contradictions of Capitalism', in Daniel Bell and Irving Kristol (eds.), *Capitalism Today,* New York: Basic Books, 1970, pp. 16-43. See also Daniel Bell, *The Cultural Contradictions of Capitalism,* New York: Basic Books, 1976, pp. 33-84.

in a more conscious fashion and on the basis of the conception of the public interest. Bell concludes that 'Inevitably a complex society, like the large, complex organizations within it, becomes a planning society'.[28] While the government in the post-industrial society can do much to contribute to the development of a communal society, Bell remains somewhat pessimistic about the possibility of creating a communal ethic that will eliminate the disjunction between a social structure that emphasizes rationality and efficiency and a counter-culture that has an antitechnological bias. His only recommendation is that men should be more modest in their utopian search for a perfect world, and that they should go more soberly about the construction of a world in which a workable balance between collective and individual action must be found.

There are many similarities between the social theorizing of Bell and other macro-sociologists and the economic theorizing of the institutionalists. They both have a systems approach which leads them to take the social system to be an evolving process; they attach considerable importance to technological change as a factor leading to changes in the social process; and they see the social process leading to the establishment of some kind of a planned society. Bell's post-industrial society has many features that are similar to the organizational society of the post-1939 institutionalists. Like Bell, Galbraith observes that the political function in society has come to dominate the economic function, as the government has expanded its controls over the private enterprise system. In the affluent industrial societies economics is undergoing a certain obsolescence as non-economic goals come to have precedence over economic goals. As Galbraith has expressed it, 'with improvement in popular well-being, economics becomes progressively more inadequate as a basis for social judgment and as a guide to public policy... With high income, questions beyond the reach of economics obtrude,' and the result is 'a disconcerting obsolescence in the profession of economics'.[29] Bell conveys the same idea by explaining that the government in the post-industrial society would move from concern with economizing to a concern with sociologizing. This sociologizing would lead to an improved life style that would be based on what Galbraith has described as 'civilized values'.

28. *The Coming of Post-Industrial Society*, p. 470.
29. *The New Industrial State*, pp. 407-8.

Both Bell and the institutionalists see the planned society of the future faced with the problems of reducing group conflict and securing more consensus or group solidarity. The obstacle to overcome is a deep separation of self from society. Bell and the institutionalists do not accept the widely-held view in sociology and economics that society is basically integral, and has an underlying unity of social structure and culture. Bell's disjunction between the social structure and culture has its counterpart in the disjunction between pecuniary and economic or technological values that is an important feature of institutionalist theorizing. Behind the institutionalists' pecuniary values is the self and its acquisitiveness, and behind their economic or technological values is society and its communal values. In the planned society of the macro-sociologists the government would seek to achieve what to the community would be a more acceptable balance between self and society. Likewise in the planned society of the institutionalists, the government would seek to achieve the production of economic values that would combine both individual and social utility.

3.8. Social sciences in the plan age

Although they do not all agree on how much importance should be attached to technological change as a factor leading to social change, many economists, sociologists, political scientists, and other social scientists now agree that technological change is an important factor resulting in social change. They also agree that scientific advance and technological change raise the two pressing problems of technological assessment and the control of technological change. Since technological change has been so rapid in recent decades and has had such profound effects on the natural and social environments, institutions, attitudes, and values, it is now clear that there is a need to assess the consequences of this change and to control the direction in which it may be leading society. Mankind now sees that it is possible to give some direction to the evolving political, social, and economic processes. The new technological age is best described as a plan age. Today all nations do some planning of their economic and social affairs. Some like the United States, Canada, West Germany and the United Kingdom under the Conservative Party plan their affairs in an informal way. Other nations like France, Belgium, The Netherlands, Norway, and Sweden plan their affairs in a formal manner by making use of indicative national planning programs based upon annual and medium-term national budgets.

An examination of the work of the sociologist Daniel Bell, the political scientist Zbigniew Brzezinski, and the economist John K. Galbraith shows that they all see the evolving social, economic, and political systems becoming parts of an overall planned society.[30] They all call for a larger perspective than the typical perspective of orthodox sociologists, political scientists, and economists. Also they all analyze the social system and its sub-systems which are in transition from one era or stage to a new era or stage. They all employ a larger dynamic framework in their analyses of the contemporary social reality than do their orthodox contemporaries. Bell, Brzezinski, and Galbraith object to the past trends in their respective social sciences that have caused them to be largely ahistorical, that have made them abstract and formal, and that have improved their technical virtuosity but at the expense of the real content of their scientific studies. As orthodox social scientists have become more technically qualified and have increasingly limited themselves to quantifiable data, they have lost what Brzezinski describes as the ability to perceive 'the broader sweep of events', and so they fail 'to develop a dynamic perspective on what is happening' in society.[31]

Bell, Brzezinski, and Galbraith believe that the emerging post-industrial society in the western world will be a participatory democracy in which interest groups will be brought closer together by the new techniques of calculation and communication. They also agree that, while groups are brought closer together on the domestic and international levels by the thrust of technological change, these groups will suffer from tensions that lead to group conflicts at home and abroad. At home class distinctions and abroad national distinctions have given rise to severe conflicts among groups in relation to such matters as income shares, civil rights, racial and ethnic discrimination, tax burdens, international competition, and the availability of the world's raw materials. To solve these conflicts and to develop a harmony of interests Bell, Brzezinski, and Galbraith call for national planning, but they offer no specifics along this line. This is not surprising since the country with

30. In this connection see Daniel Bell, 'Introduction', in Herman Kahn and Anthony J. Wiener, *The Year 2000,* New York: Macmillan, 1967, p. xxv; John Kenneth Galbraith, *Economics and the Public Purpose,* p. 318; and Zbigniew Brzezinski, *Between Two Ages, America's Role in the Technetronic Era,* New York: Viking Press, 1970, p. 61.
31. *Between Two Ages,* p. xiv.

which they are most familiar, namely, the United States, does not engage in any formal type of national planning. The United States has been the principal disseminator of the scientific-technological revolution, but it has not had the same role with respect to social and economic institutional innovation. In national, regional, and urban planning the United States has much to learn from Western Europe.

Two major issues of the final quarter of this century will be the determination of national goals and priorities and the creation of an effective incomes policy.[32] Both of these issues are much more than economic issues. They cut across the fields of economics, sociology, political science, and social psychology, and they raise complicated questions of new institutional arrangements, new attitudes, and new values. We have made very limited progress with respect to these two important matters, especially in the United States, because the various social sciences have failed to work cooperatively when faced with these issues. All too frequently the economist, when confronted with these problems, argues that they should be taken care of by the political scientist or some other social scientist. Likewise, the political scientist has too frequently said that these issues more properly belong in the field of economics or sociology. The net result is that much too little work has been done in the various social sciences on these very crucial problems.

Bell, Brzezinski, Galbraith, and other American social scientists have to look to Western Europe for examples of successful democratic national planning. National planning in France, Sweden, and other planned countries includes both economic and social planning. It brings together the nation's interest groups and provides an open forum for the discussion of the aspirations and needs of these various groups. The national budget, which shows the claims of all interest groups on the nation's gross national product, is the focal point of all indicative national planning programs. The determination of national goals and priorities through the political process and their harmonization with the aid of the national budget make use of the expertise of many social scientists. It is at this point that the interdisciplinary approach has much to offer, and that social science experts can contribute a great deal.

National planning can contribute to the fashioning of a new set of

32. These two major issues are discussed in Allan G. Gruchy, 'Whither Neo-institutionalism? An Analysis of Its Trends and Prospects', *Rocky Mountain Social Science Journal*, Vol. 12, April, 1975, pp. 49-58.

national values, and to the development of a communal ethic without which the post-industrial society cannot provide a satisfactory life style. National planning, however, is not a panacea for all of society's problems. It does not guarantee that the disjunction between the social structure and culture to which Bell has referred will be eliminated. Nor does national planning guarantee that a new communal ethic will arise to provide a common framework of values for the nation's different economic interest groups that can guide the setting of national goals and priorities. What democratic national planning does is to bring together the nation's various interest groups with the aid of a program for joint consultation. This planning also provides a way of discussing the goals, attitudes, and values of these various groups and the constraints within which these matters should be analyzed. National planning is a means of achieving satisfactory balances between personal freedom and community order, and between social continuity and change. Securing these two balances requires that in this current era of historic transition we adopt an anticipatory method of dealing with economic and social problems.[33] Up to now we have too frequently clung to a reactive method of handling these problems, which has induced us to wait until these problems have forced themselves upon us before doing anything about them. If we are going to be more systematic and rational in assessing national goals, our decision making process has to be more effectively planned. Decision making within a democratically planned framework emphasizes the importance of an anticipatory approach which leads us to prepare for problems before they emerge. The anticipatory approach also lays stress on what Myrdal describes as the 'long view' in which the alternative futures that are open to us are analyzed before a decision is made to follow a particular course. Any such anticipatory approach to national desicion making, if it is to be effective, requires the cooperation of many social scientists and the development of a multidisciplinary approach to the handling of the problems of the emerging post-industrial society.

3.9. The integration of the social sciences

Institutional economics concerns itself with more than the usual matters of interest to orthodox or micro-macroeconomists. Since institutional

33. Report of the National Goals Staff, *Toward Balanced Growth: Quantity with Quality*, Washington, D.C., 1970, pp. 27-37.

economics deals with the evolving economic system, it raises questions that Robert A. Gordon has described as 'the big questions about how and why the institutional structure is changing – and where it is taking us'.[34] By relating the market mechanism to the institutional structure surrounding it the institutionalists bring to the front such questions as economic efficiency for whose benefit and for what purposes, and also why income and wealth are distributed among individuals in the ways they actually are. On a broader front, the institutionalists, like Marx, ask: where is the capitalist economy going and why?

When broadening the scope of economics in this manner, the institutionalists investigate the economic system, the social or cultural system in which the economic system is embedded, and the political system which greatly affects the process of economic decision making. In his work of analyzing the evolving capitalist system the institutionalist borrows heavily from the sociologists and cultural anthropologists whose theory of culture explains the social system, and from the political scientists who explain the political process and how it resolves problems of group or class conflict. The theory of culture of the sociologists has much to say about scientific and technological advances and their impacts on the social system, the class structure and its related power system, values and their role in the unfolding of the human personality, and the logic or pattern of cultural development. All these matters are found to be of great value by the institutionalist in his analysis of the evolving capitalist system. The political scientist explains the role of government in the capitalist system, the competition among groups to acquire political influence or power, and the ways in which the government system operates in the areas of public choice and public goods. As in the case of sociology, the institutionalist finds much in the area of political science that is helpful in revealing the nature of the western industrial democracies.

Social scientists, who wish to be realistic and who wish to deal with the real world around them, find it is essential to be informed about three areas of scientific interest, namely, the economy, the social or cultural

34. Robert Aaron Gordon, 'Rigor and Relevance in a Changing Institutional Setting', *American Economic Review,* Vol. 66, March 1976, p. 1. In his presidential address to the American Economic Association at Dallas, Texas, in Dec. 1975 Gordon asked the same questions that the institutionalists have asked: 'How did we get to where we are, and where are we going? Or, if you will, what is the future of capitalism and the kind of market economy to which we are accustomed and which is changing before our eyes?' (p. 11).

system, and the political system. What differentiates one social scientist from another is the different emphasis that he places upon the three areas of interest listed above. The interdisciplinary sociologist makes the social or cultural system his main concern, with the other two scientific areas being ancillary or secondary. The interdisciplinary political scientist makes the political process his main concern, with the economy and the cultural system being supplementary to his main field of interest. The interdisciplinary economist in his own way relates his primary field, the economic process, to the cultural and political processes.

Economists, sociologists, and political scientists in the West are analyzing the same capitalist system but from different perspectives. The capitalist system of Western Europe and the United States is a democratic system with a set of western individualistic values and a mixed private-public enterprise economy. It is to be distinguished from the economic system of Eastern Europe with its undemocratic system, collectivistic values, and state-operated economy. What western social scientists have in common is an interest in a particular social system, one that has a democratic political structure, cultural values that stress individual welfare as an ultimate concern, and a mixed private-public enterprise economy such as is found in all the West European democracies. It is this common view of the evolving advanced industrial society that fosters the interdisciplinary approach among realistic economists, sociologists, and political scientists. This common view prepares these social scientists to cope with the major economic and social problems of the final quarter of the twentieth century, – problems that are in large part beyond the analytical grasp of orthodox economists.

4. In defense of institutionalism

K. William Kapp†

'I see the tasks of social sciences to discover what kinds of order actually do exist in the whole range of the behavior of human beings; what kind of functional relationships between different parts of culture exist in space and over time, and what functionally more useful kinds of order can be created.' R.S. Lynd, *Knowledge for What?*, 1939, pp. 125/26.

'The failure of the social sciences to think through and to integrate their several responsibilities for the common problem of relating the analysis of parts to the analysis of the whole constitutes one of the major lags crippling their utility as human tools of knowledge...', *Ibid.*, p. 15.

4.1. Introduction

Robert Lynd's critical diagnosis of the crippling situation of the social sciences in the thirties was echoed later by Schumpeter's statement that the social sciences have steadily grown apart 'until by now the modal economist and the modal sociologist know little and care less about what the other does, each preferring to use, respectively, a primitive sociology and a primitive economics of his own to accepting one anothers' professional results – a state of things that was and is not improved by mutual vituperation'.[1]

In fact, neo-classical[2] economics has tended increasingly to develop into a self-contained body of knowledge which has become more and more isolated from other social sciences and analytical systems. This has been brought about by the influence of several inter-related tendencies and orientations which cannot be examined here as thoroughly as would be desirable. No doubt, the mathematization and formalization of economic theory have played a predominant role. So has a methodologi-

1. Joseph A. Schumpeter, *History of Economic Analysis*, New York, Oxford University Press, 1955, p. 26/27.
2. The term 'neo-classical' is used here in a broad sense including standard micro- and macro-economics.

cal individualism which can be traced back to the origins of our discipline. Equally important is the long tradition of reasoning by analogy to mechanics and the related research for levels of stable equilibrium as well as the implicitly normative insistence that economic theory is concerned with the explication of the logic of rational action under conditions of scarcity or, as Lionel Robbins, following P.H. Wicksteed, put it, with a particular type or 'form' of human conduct: the study of 'human behavior as a relationship between ends and means which have alternative uses'.[3]

Under the influence of these orientations conventional economic theory has defined its subject-matter and the scope of its analysis in a rather narrow way and has convinced its practitioners that it is possible and useful to distinguish between 'economic' and 'non-economic' factors or aspects of social processes. Concrete economic systems or processes are thus believed to be adequately represented as isolated, self-contained and self-sustaining, closed mechanical processes with definable boundaries.

While it is true that individual economists who laid the foundation of neo-classical analysis have repeatedly and explicitly warned against any belief in the 'self-sufficiency' of neo-classical analysis particularly for the formulation of practical policies[4] the mainstream of neo-classicism has not heeded these warnings and has instead insisted on the autonomy and greater specialization of economic analysis if not its systematic isolation from other social sciences. A few illustrations may suffice to illustrate this point. Schumpeter denied the relevance of psychology for economic theorizing by stating, without qualifications and apparently with approval, that 'economists have never allowed their analysis to be influenced by psychologists of their time, but have always framed for themselves such assumptions about psychical processes as they have thought it

3. Lionel Robbins, *The Nature and Significance of Economic Science*, London, Macmillan & Co., 1932, p. 16. Wicksteed had pointed out that 'there is no occasion to define the economic motive, or the psychology of the economic man, for 'economics study a type of relation, not a type of motive and the psychological law that dominates economics dominates life'. P.H. Wicksteed, The Scope and Method of Political Economy in the Light of the Marginal Theory of Value and Distribution, *Economic Journal*, Vol. 24, 1914, p. 10.
4. Thus Wicksteed stated explicitly 'that the economic machine is constructed and moved by individuals for individual ends, and that its social effect is incidental...', 'that the market does not tell us in any fruitful sense what are the "national", "social" and "collective" wants'..., that 'economic laws must not be sought and cannot be found on the properly economic field...', that 'to recognize this will be to humanize economics...', and 'that economics must be the handmaid of sociology', Philip H. Wicksteed, *op. cit.*, p. 11-12.

desirable to make'.[5] Duesenbery who rediscovered what he called the (Veblenian) demonstration effect defended the neglect of psychology 'as a deliberate attempt to sidestep the tasks of making psychological assumptions... (which) has the advantage that it allows one to avoid getting out on a psychological limb which may collapse at any moment'.[6] Other neo-classical economists were even more explicit in rejecting attempts to relate economic analysis to other social disciplines. Thus, in opposing the trend toward interdisciplinary studies at American universities, G.J. Stigler dissented by stating categorically that the royal road of efficiency in intellectual as in economic life is specialism – not interdisciplinary work.[7]

These attitudes together with the orientations outlined above have tended to push conventional economic theory more and more into the direction of a formal, self-contained, closed mechanical analytical system and have prevented the assimilation of new perspectives and new paradigms developed by other disciplines. In fact, we seem to be witnessing to-day the extension of the neo-classical theoretical framework to such fields as the analysis of political behavior, public choice, and decision-making in general. While this development may be regarded by some as a move in the direction of inter-disciplinarity it carries with it the dangers of a new kind of reductionism of social analysis to neo-classicism. It is not too late that social scientists and sociologists in particular take a critical position toward this kind of 'academic imperialism'.[8]

4.2. Institutional economics

Dissatisfaction with the 'mechanics of utility and self-interest'[9] and the narrow scope of conventional economics manifested itself very early; in fact, criticism has never ceased and is to-day stronger than ever. As

5. Joseph A. Schumpeter, *op.cit.*, p. 27.
6. J.S. Duesenbery, Income, Savings and the Theory of Consumers Behavior, Cambridge, Harvard University Press, 1949, p. 15.
7. G.J. Stigler, Specialism: A Dissenting Opinion, *Bulletin* (Am. Ass. of University Professors), Winter 1951/52, p.30.
8. Brian M. Barry, Sociologists, Economists and Democracy, London, Collier Macmillan Ltd., 1970.
9. The words are those of W. Stanley Jevons, see his Theory of Political Economy, 2nd edition, London, Macmillan, 1879, p. 23.

always in times of economic and social crisis 'normal' economic theory is under attack and is criticized for its inability to provide an appropriate analytical framework for the diagnosis of the problems and the formulation of more adequate criteria, policies and remedies designed to cope with increasing internal and international disparities, environmental disruption, stagnation and inflation as well as unemployment, conflicts over terms of trade, etc.

The critique has always been directed against the scope and methodological preconceptions inherent in the equilibrium approach. This holds true for the historical school; it applies to Marx (with some qualifications) and to institutional economics the origins of which go back to the early critics of classical economics. What these critics have in common is the denial that economic processes (of production, distribution, and reproduction) can be adequately understood and analysed as closed, i.e. self-contained and self-sustaining systems isolated from a social and physical 'environment' of which the economic system is a part and from which it receives important inputs and with which it is related through manifold reciprocal interdependencies. In other words, the critics have always considered the economy as an open system in continuous dynamic interaction with a more comprehensive social and political as well as physical system from which economic processes receive important organising (and disorganising) impulses and upon which they exert their own negative and positive influences. In addition to denying the self-contained and self-sustaining character of economic processes and by stressing the open character of economic systems the critics have challenged above all the belief in the mechanical and self-regulating character of economic processes. They have questioned the search for levels of partial and total equilibrium within an artificially closed system; they have refused to accept the view that economic analysis must confine itself to the study of a particular type or form of behavior; that the best method of studying complex phenomena is to separate the parts and study them one by one,[10] and that specialism is the royal road to efficiency in social analysis. In short, the critics have always been more or less open to other social and natural sciences. This applies particularly to institutional economists.

In fact, institutional economics has always aimed at a coherent representation of economic processes as part of a complex social system

10. Vilfredo Pareto, Traité de Sociologie Générale, Lausanne, Librairie Payot, 1917, p. 17.

and their interaction. Institutionalists have endeavored to make explicit the relationships and the reciprocal interaction of the parts with one another and with the 'whole'. Long before structuralism and functionalism appeared on the academic horizon institutionalists have placed this reciprocal interaction in the center of their theoretical investigations. Institutionalists have found it problematical and indeed unacceptable to draw classificatory distinctions between so-called economic and non-economic factors and between economic and social processes. In order to illustrate these important characteristics of institutional economics let me first contrast Robbins' definition of economics with Gruchy's characterisation of institutional (or evolutionary) economics. According to Gruchy economics is concerned with 'the study of the structure and functioning of the *evolving* field of human relations which is concerned with the provision of material goods and services for the satisfaction of human wants. ... it is the study of the changing patterns of cultural relations which deals with the creation and disposal of scarce material goods and services by individuals and *groups* in the light of their private and *public* aims'.[11] Hence, whereas the neo-classical definition selects rational human conduct as a criterion Gruchy makes it clear that economics is concerned with a much broader range of problems, namely the interdependencies of a great number of variables within a dynamic process of human and socio-cultural (interpersonal) relations which result from changing modes of production, distribution and social reproduction. Not a particular *form* of behavior serves as the criterion of differentiation of economic analysis and determines its scope and approach but rather a particular set of interconnected dynamic problems which arise in the satisfaction of individual needs and public objectives.

In fact, the institutional approach focusses attention on the evolution of social systems and social processes. The analysis of the factors which provide the dynamic elements of these evolutionary processes has been in the center of institutional economics. Thus innovations, science and technologies as well as conflicts of interests, power and coercion in economic and social life have therefore always been included in their investigations. The central role of science, technology and innovations found an early expression in Veblen's *Theory of Business Enterprise* (1904). 'The material framework of modern civilization is the industrial

11. A.G. Gruchy, *Modern Economic Thought*, New York, Prentice Hall, 1947, pp. 550, 552 (emphasis added).

system, and the directing force which animates this framework is business enterprise... This modern economic organization of the 'Capitalistic System' or 'Modern Industrial System' so-called, its characteristic features, and at the same time, the forces by virtue of which it dominates modern culture, are the machine process and investment for a profit'.[12] Innovation, technology and domination of economic processes by the machine process set the pace for the rest of the industrial system and distinguish the present situation from all previous forms of economic organizations and civilizations. The aim of institutional economics is 'a theory of business enterprise... sufficiently full to show in what manner business methods and business principles, in conjunction with the mechanical industry, influence the modern cultural situation'.[13]

In addition, Veblen's theory of business enterprise laid the foundation for the analysis of economic instability and business fluctuations with their cumulative processes of investment based upon credit and the pervasive creation of debts, the generation of demand and employment and 'the inflation of all monetary values'.

The preoccupation with the role of conflict, power and coercion is an intellectual heritage which, in America, antedates Marx and goes back to the Federalists and their European mentors prior to the American Revolution; early American institutionalists like Veblen and Commons have reformulated and integrated this heritage into their analysis of 'vested interests', absentee ownership, the economic role of the state, the legal foundations of capitalism, the importance of collective and political bargaining, public utility regulations and the analysis of collusion between financial, industrial and political power. In short, the problems raised by the industrial military complex and the 'power elite' have not been neglected in institutional economics.

In harmony with their early critique of the classical preconceptions and particularly the mechanics of self-interests developed by neo-classical utility price and equilibrium theory, institutional economists have from the very beginning been sceptical of market prices in terms of which business enterprise tends to measure its performance and efficiency in utilizing scarce resources, i.e. of the criteria which price

12. Thorstein Veblen, *The Theory of Business Enterprise*, New York, Charles Scriener's Sons, 1904, p. 1.

13. *Ibid.*, p.21. For an account of the emergence of innovations and new technologies, cf. Veblen's *Instinct of Workmanship and the State of The Industrial Arts*, New York, 1914.

theory has accepted and legitimized, at least until quite recently, as criteria of optimal decision-making and as indicators of economic rationality in general. No wonder, therefore, that institutional economists were among the first who have called attention to and have analysed in considerable detail the social costs of production, long before the latter found a sudden and belated recognition in the current discussion of the increasing environmental and ecological disruption (including the exhaustion of non-renewable stock resources) with its serious threats to social reproduction and the quality of individual and social life. Unlike positive economics, institutional economists have not hesitated to use the results of their inquiries as the basis of a critique of existing institutions and the *status quo*.

Equally significant have been the contributions of institutionalists to the analysis of underdevelopment (and development) and the persistence of increasing disparities not only between rich and poor countries but also within each of these two groups. Myrdal's seminal studies of underdevelopment in South East Asia just as his earlier work on race problems in America are the outstanding examples of an institutional analysis which has overcome the conventional concentration on 'economic' variables such as savings and investment, employment, money, interest rates and G.N.P. Myrdal and others have shown the true dimension and complexity of the persistent problems of poverty and underdevelopment and their relation to institutions, the soft state, the fundamental issue of the relationships between man and land including land-tenure relationships,[14] the population-resources relationship, illiteracy, the low level and an appropriate content of education, poor health and nutrition, pre-scientific knowledge of techniques, traditional attitudes, value systems, class, caste and kinship systems, and, last but not least, the domination effect (Perroux) and center-periphery problem (Galtung) with its farreaching effects on the terms of trade. All these problems neo-classical theory had pushed more or less aside; to-day (1975) they can no longer be ignored for the simple reason that the countries of the Third World have begun to insist upon a new world economic order. No analysis in purely economic terms which abstracts from these institutional factors is able to come to terms with the circular interdependencies between these factors and the cumulative causal interaction which delay and arrest the process of development.

14. Erich Jacoby (with Charlotte Jacoby), *Man and Land*, London, André Deutsch, 1971

The preoccupation with problems of the kind outlined above gives institutional economics its scope and shows why there have always existed points of contact with other social and natural sciences including sociology, social anthropology, political science and ecology.

Needless to add that sociologists, social anthropologists and political scientists have contributed in no small measure to our understanding of such important elements of the development process as the analysis of caste, kinship and religion, factions and class conflict in traditional village life, attitudes and responses to innovation and modernization, economic motivation in traditional rural societies and socio-cultural evolution in general. However, in contrast to institutional economists these other social scientists have found it difficult, until quite recently, 'to think in terms of planning for national development. They are still laboring with finding out how people live and survive, and they are regularly, different from other economists, dealing with only segments of the national society and also mostly focussing their work on certain problems that have traditionally been at the center of their attention like e.g. caste in India. They have seldom attempted systematically to lay bare the circular causation between all conditions in a society they are studying'.[15]

4.3. The principle of interlocking interdependencies within a process of cumulative causation as a new theoretical framework for the solution of concrete problems

With Myrdal's formulation of the principle of circular causation we finally arrive at the core of institutional economics which sets it apart from earlier and contemporary non-institutionalist approaches and particularly from mecnanistic equilibrium analysis. For, 'the principle of interlocking circular interdependencies within a process of cumulative causation'[16] is at the same time a new theoretical framework which rejects and replaces the traditional equilibrium framework and an analytical tool which permits the solution of concrete problems (i.e. of problematical, indeterminate situations) which have, so far, remained

15. Gunnar Myrdal, *The Unity of the Social Sciences,* Planory Addressed to the Society of Applied Anthropology, Amsterdam, March 21, 1975 (ms), p. 12.
16. Gunnar Myrdal, *Economic Theory and Underdeveloped Regions,* London, Gerald Duckworth & Co., 1957, p. 23.

anomalies which could not be adequately accounted for in terms of the traditional 'disciplinary matrix'.[17]

The principle of interlocking circular interdependencies within a process of cumulative causation has a long history. It played an important role in Malthus' analysis of the growth and decline of populations. Thünen advanced an early version of it when he stated that the manual worker cannot rise into the class of enterpreneurs because he lacks the necessary schooling because wages are low which, in turn, is due to the fact that the poor have higher reproduction rates and hence the supply of labor is almost always higher than the demand, and consequently wages tend towards the subsistence level.[18] Marx was the first to stress the fundamental reciprocal interaction between 'productive forces' and 'production relations' and the ideological superstructure. Veblen developed and used the principle of circular interdependencies of a number of factors within a process of cumulative causation in connection with his analysis of the function of the leisure class, the role of technology and credit particularly in connection with his explanation of the business cycle and the 'inflation of all monetary values'; and so did Knut Wicksel, within a narrower market framework, in his account of the inflationary expansion of credit resulting from a deviation of the money (market) interest rate from the natural, real rate of interest.[19]

However, it was left to Myrdal to develop the principle of interlocking interdependencies within a process of cumulative causation in a

17. I am using here Thomas Kuhn's *new* terminus instead of his earlier 'paradigm'. Following Margaret Masterman, Kuhn now identifies the growth of knowledge with 'framework breaking' whereby the 'traditional framework of analysis for problems solving (disciplinary matrix) is rejected *and* replaced by another set of ordered elements capable of 'solving' or accounting for what remained unexplained by the former: 'an artifact which transforms problems to puzzles and enables them to be solved even in the absence of an adequate body of theory'. Thomas Kuhn, Reflections on my Critics, in: Imre Lakatos and Alan Musgrave (eds.), *Criticism and the Growth of Knowledge,* Cambridge, at the University Press, 1970, p. 273. Cf. also Margaret Masterman, The Nature of a Paradigm, *Ibid.,* p. 59-90.

18. Johann H. von Thünen, *Der Isolierte Staat* (1850), Jena, Gustav Fischer, 1910, p. 440/41.

19. The neo-classical theoretical framework of general equilibrium or total interdependence of all prices in a market economy is of course also a case of mutual interlocking interdependencies. However, in contrast to Veblen and Myrdal, the neo-classical framework postulates an isolated closed analytical model with self-equilibrating tendencies. Similarly the 'multiplier' or the 'accelerator' are cases of cumulative interdependencies even though the relationship referred to are conceived in a narrow mechanical and deterministic fashion.

systematic way, and to have shown its significance and its implications as an alternative analytical framework for the entire field of social relations. He has done this in a continuous critical confrontation with the closed system of neo-classical equilibrium analysis, its hidden political or normative elements and in his life-long preoccupation with concrete and persistent problems such as race discrimination in America, international disparities, and the intractable problems of underdevelopment and poverty in Asia. In dealing with these problems Myrdal has developed a new explanatory theoretical framework which consist of a matrix of ordered and specified elements of social conditions which, in their reciprocal interdependence, can be shown to influence the evolution and transformation of social processes. As an examplary illustration we choose the relationship between developed and underdeveloped countries and the interpretation of the process of development and underdevelopment. The problems to be accounted for are the empirically observed disparities and the persistence of development differentials between 'rich' and 'poor' countries or regions. Both rich and poor regions are characterized by a number of specific conditions which can be classified or categorized in different ways. Myrdal considers the following conditions as relevant for the analysis and interpretation of the process of underdevelopment: *Productivity* (output/worker; income population); *conditions of production* (techniques, scale, capital intensity, savings and investment, social overhead, labor utilization and employment); *levels of living* (nutrition, housing, hygiene, medical attention, education and training, literacy and income distribution); *attitudes* to production, work and living (discipline, punctuality, prejudice, apathy, world outlooks, religion, absence of birth control, etc.); *institutions* (man-land relations, tenure conditions, market structures, class, caste and kinship systems, structure of national and local government and administration, etc.) and *policies and legislation* (the 'soft state', lack of law enforcement, taxation, mobilization of savings). Needless to say, this does not represent a complete list of possible relevant factors and conditions; moreover, they may have to be classified in a different manner depending upon problems and regions to be investigated. However, the important point is that, among all the conditions, there exists a causal relationship, and this relationship is to a large extent, but not always, of a circular character. In other words, the principle of circular interdependencies postulates a mutual responsiveness, i.e. a capacity of the different conditions to react upon changes of one or several elements. It is this circular and cumulative interaction which determines the dynamics of the system which institutional analysis has to elucidate and to determine. In addition, it is essential to study the specific circular interrelations between the different factors and conditions before it will be possible to define objectives, to develop appropriate criteria of choice, and to make decisions with regard to long-run strategies as well as specific developmental policies. For, the formulation of such strategies and policies will require detailed, regional and local empirical studies designed to ascertain the concrete relationships between the different endogenous factors and conditions including their responsiveness to one another as well as the possible time lags and, in some cases, the lack of responsiveness of one or several of them to induced changes initiated by policy measures.[20]

In other words, only by ascertaining the interaction and responsiveness of productivity and conditions of production to changes of the level of living, institutions and policy measures, it is possible to arrive at reasonable judgments as to the possible effects and outcomes of alternative policies, investments, and legislative action, as for instance agrarian reforms, new techniques, etc. In this sense, we believe that it is justified to regard the principle of interlocking circular interdependencies within a process of cumulative causation as the 'disciplinary matrix' which provides institutional economists with a new tool for the identification and ordering of the relevant elements in the study of socio-economic processes in their immensely diversified and changing complexity. More than this, the principle enables institutionalists (and other social scientists) to transform problematical situations and unsolved open problems (as for instance increasing disparities within and between 'rich' and 'poor' regions) into 'puzzles' which can be solved even when a complete theory and the precise knowledge as to the 'coefficients of interaction' are not (yet) available. As a matter of fact, this is precisely what the principle of circular interdependencies has made possible not only with regard to the 'diagnostic' identification of relevant factors and conditions with regard to the problem of underdevelopment, but also with respect to the specification of possible measures and priorities required to deal with them.

One thing deserves special emphasis before turning to other matters. This is the question of the boundaries of the system and hence the

20. Gunnar Myrdal, The Unity of the Social Sciences, *op. cit.*, p. 6.

question of the limits of the analysis. In other words, how far and how wide have we to extend the net of our investigations? A general but perhaps not entirely satisfactory answer is that all factors which can be shown to have a possible influence on the process or problem under investigation will have to be included regardless of whether or not this transcends the borderlines between traditional academic disciplines. In a more fundamental sense, the answer to the question as to the boundary of the system and hence to the factors to be included depends on the nature of the problem and the purpose of the investigation. The recent emergence of environmental disruption, the increase of oil prices, and the problems of energy and other non-renewable resources force economists to realize that economic processes depend upon a continuous exchange of energy and matter between the economy and nature and that available and accessible matter-energy is continuously and irreversibly transformed and partly dissipated into unavailable energy (increasing entropy). Therefore, an adequate and complete analytical description of economic processes cannot be obtained by the analysis of closed system (e.g. circulatory processes of production and consumption or systems of partial and total equilibrium, etc.) but calls for a representation of what the process needs in the form of input and what it does to man's environment by the emission of pollutants and the disposal of waste material. In other words, what is called for is a specification of the inputs required (and available), of the outputs including wastes disposed into the environment; the energy required (and available) for the transformation process as well as the resulting qualitative changes in time and space. I am listing these points not in order to suggest that institutional economics has already solved these problems but rather in order to call attention to the wide gap which exists between economic reality and the economic models currently used for the theoretical representation of economic processes. In short, the question of the boundary of the system raises much more fundamental problems than is usually believed; it includes the problem of the relevant time horizon or, more precisely, the question of the appropriate long-run time schedules of the inputs and outputs to be considered.[21] One thing, however, should be clear from the

21. '...where we draw the abstract boundary, what duration we consider, and what qualitative spectrum we use for classifying the elements of the process depends on the particular purpose of the student, and by and large on the science in point'. Nicholas Georgescu-Roegen, Energy and Economic Myths, *Southern Economic Journal,* Vol. 41, No. 3, January 1975, p. 350.

foregoing observations: the existing borderlines between traditional disciplines are to-day the most important obstacles to an adequate analytical treatment of economic and social processes. This is the essential point of Myrdal's dictum: there are no economic (or, for that matter, sociological) problems; there are only problems and they are all complex. In fact, Myrdal recently made the point that since research must be focussed on specific problems which are all composite and mixed, 'borderlines between our traditional disciplines should be transgressed systematically'.[22]

The central significance of the principle of circular interdependencies and cumulative causation derives from the fact that it abandons and, in fact, explicitly rejects the notion of stable equilibrium as a misleading and unwarranted analogy to mechanics. From the perspective of mechanics everything is treated as a pendular movement where changes produce their counterbalancing forces and where production merely becomes a process of transformation under the influence of a maximization rule.[23] 'Actually, the economic process is not an isolated, self-sustaining process. It cannot go on without a continuous exchange which alters the environment in a cumulative way and without being, in its turn, influenced by these alterations'.[24]

In short, economic processes can be understood and must be represented for analytical purposes as radically open systems which exchange energy and matter with the environment in the course of which qualitative changes take place both with respect to the environment and the process itself. That is to say, socio-economic processes move in a definite direction and this direction needs to be ascertained.[25]

However, even if we could get away from the fundamental fact of entropy the analogy to mechanics with the notion of stable equilibrium would still be problematical and usually misleading for the analysis of contemporary social conditions. For, these conditions are no longer, if they ever were, characterized by the interaction of a great number of more or less equal units in perfect competition none of which exert a

22. Gunnar Myrdal, The Unity of the Social Sciences, *op. cit.*, p. 15.
23. 'To equate the economic process with a mechanical analogue implies... the myth that the economic process is a circular merry-go-round which cannot possibly affect the environment of matter and energy in any way'. Georgescu-Roegen, *op.cit.*, p. 350.
24. *Ibid.*, p. 348.
25. 'Actual phenomena move in a definite direction and involve qualitative change. This is the lesson of thermodynamics... (i.e. the law of increasing entropy or the continuous dissipation of available energy into unavailable energy). *Ibid.*, p. 351/52.

dominating influence on the direction of the process and its outcome (e.g. prices, quantities produced and sold, inputs chosen, technologies adopted, and location selected). Exchanges between dominating and dominated units, give rise to unequal exchanges and unequal terms of trade and to a choice of inputs, technologies and locations which are bound to result in self-reinforcing movements and an unequal distribution of income, growing disparities and polarization . In short, in the normal course of exchange relations between dominating and dominated units, between 'center' and 'periphery', between 'growth poles' and dependent economies there is no assurance that inequalities and domination will cease or 'backwash' effects will be compensated by expansionary 'spread' effects.

Under these circumstances, it becomes clear why the new theoretical framework of circular interdependence and cumulative causation is justified to reject the analogy to mechanics with its notion of stable equilibrium as a paradigm of problem solving in the social sciences. In fact, the new paradigm assumes that 'the system is by itself not moving towards any sort of balance between forces, but is constantly on the move away from such a situation. In the normal case a change does not call for countervailing changes but, instead, supporting changes, which move the system in the same direction as the first change but much further. Because of such circular causation a social process tends to become cumulative and often to gather speed at an accelerating rate'.[26] The principle does not prejudge the direction of the cumulative response nor the final outcome. In fact, it does *not* imply only 'vicious' circles. In other words, the response of the system to an endogenous or exogenous change such as deliberately planned exogenous impulses may either reinforce, retard or reverse the process; hence there is room for a variety of possibilities of interdependencies.[27]

Moreover, the principle of cumulative causation and circular interdependencies offers a logical explanation why, under certain conditions, relatively 'small' changes are capable of bringing about comparatively 'big' effects of transformations in socio-economic as well as ecological processes. Once the conditions for cumulative processes (either upward or downward) exist in a particular system a relatively small additional impulse can act as an 'evocator' of substantial, non-linear and even

26. Gunnar Myrdal, *Economic Theory and Underdeveloped Regions, op.cit.*, p. 13.
27. Gunnar Myrdal, *Asian Drama*, Vol. III, New York, Pantheon Books, 1968, p. 1859.

'jump-like' transformations particularly when certain limits or thresh-holds of tolerance are reached. Good examples for such disproportionalities between cause and effect can be found in the field of air and water pollution where the carrying capacity of the environment may be reached or exceeded by small additional emissions of pollutants. Needless to add the principle of the disproportionality between cause and effect is not confined to environmental disruption. It applies also to socio-economic as well as to biological processes as it does to chemico-physical reactions.

Before concluding these considerations let me come back to the problem of the precision and completeness of our knowledge regarding cumulative causation and circular interdependencies of a great number of conditions. I have already referred to 'coefficients of interaction' of relevant variables, to possible time lags, and even to the total non-responsiveness of one or several of the relevant conditions to induced changes. Institutional economists are not opposed to precise and quantitative knowledge; on the contrary, they were among the first to call for and insist upon the quantification of relevant relationships between variables in scientific investigations.[28] They have insisted on precise concept formations as well as on detailed and disaggregated empirical and quantitative statistical studies of all important factors and their *interaction* irrespective of conventional borderlines between academic disciplines with a view to filling the gaps of our knowledge. But, unlike those who are interested in quantification and precision out of a 'quest for certainty' and a search for precise and purely formal solutions of frequently esoteric problems, institutionalists have remained aware of and have warned against the tendency 'to overlook the imperfection of our knowledge and to pretend to precise knowledge which does not stand scrutiny' and serve no rational purpose.[29] While the ideal scientific solution of a problem may be, as Myrdal indicated, to formulate 'an interconnected set of quantitative equations, describing the movement – and the internal changes – of the system under the various influences which are at work'[30] such a quantitative formulation is to-day, as Myrdal also pointed out, far beyond the horizon. Moreover, I doubt

28. Cf. W.E. Mitchell's work on business cycles and his programmatic article, Quantitative Analysis in Economic Analysis, *The American Economic Review*, Vol. XV, March 1925. Myrdal was one of the founder members of the Econometric Society.
29. Gunnar Myrdal, *The Unity of the Social Sciences*, *op.cit.*, p. 6.
30. Gunnar Myrdal, *Economic Theory and Underdeveloped Regions*, *op.cit.*, p. 19.

that we possess or will ever possess the data and the type of mathematics needed for the quantitative formulation of mutual circular interdependencies and thus for a precise expression of coefficients of interaction. In any event, it would be questionable if not illogical to require, or to make action dependent upon, a degree of quantitative precision of our knowledge which may be neither attainable nor necessary for the formulation of social policies.

4.4. Some practical implications of the principle of circular interdependencies

In rejecting the mechanical equilibrium approach as false and misleading and by stressing the importance of the principle of circular causation institutionalists do not argue that the situation is hopeless. While it is true that institutionalists regard circular causation, disruption, disparities and disequilibria as normal tendencies they also regard these tendencies as the main determinants of the dynamics of the system, both evolutionary and cataclysmic.[31] At the same time, it is these dynamic tendencies towards disequilibrium which provide the main impulse for attempts at remedying, channelling and controlling social and economic processes by deliberate policy measures with a view to maintaining social reproduction.

What should be the specific policy objectives of such measures? How will they be determined? How can they be defined? Which criteria need to be used? These are some of the central questions with which institutionalists will have to concern themselves. They have only begun to deal with these problems and it would be too much to expect that a large measure of agreement has been reached, except at the most general level. Myrdal, in his studies of underdevelopment, speaks of modernization ideals and economic integration as goals of policies designed to guide the process of development planning with a view to moving the entire social system 'upwards'.[32]

31. W.F. Wertheim, Evolution and Revolution, Harmondsworth, Penguin Book, 1974.

32. Myrdal's modernization ideals are the basic and explicit value premises underlying the development effort; they include social and economic equalization, greater rationality, improved levels of living, including nutrition, health and housing, rise of productivity, new institutions, attitudes and motivations including the liberation from all notions of fatalism and 'destiny', national consolidation, self-reliance. These ideals have been criticized as

Others have argued that balanced growth be considered as a general objective of policy measures particularly in developed countries. This advances us only in so far as it stresses the need to look for, and to develop appropriate criteria and definitions of states of dynamic equilibria which should be the basis for the formulation of the specific goals and objectives of all our strategies and policies in a world in which tendencies toward disequilibrium are typical and prevailing whereas conditions of equilibrium and balance are transitory and provisional. In this sense and in so far as unbalance and disequilibrium endanger social reproduction and hence human life and survival, the analysis of disequilibria and the search for dynamic states of balance as policy objectives may indeed be said to be complementary. The latter presupposes the former.

However, I would go one step further. The search for and hence the formulation of conditions of admittedly transitory balance and equilibrium will have to be guided not only by a critical and diagnostic identification of the full range of relevant variables, their circular interaction and their logical (probable) outcome but by fundamental and explicit value premises. For to avoid value judgments in the field of practical action in an effort of maintaining one's alleged objectivity is nothing but an evasion of the basic problems inherent in policy formulation. In order to contribute to the latter social inquiry must go beyond a purely positive analysis of the interaction of relevant variables; it will have to assess critically the outcome of social processes *in the absence* of deliberate social action and, in the light of such a critical evaluation of reality, contribute to what may be called the formulation of

eurocentric and 'Western' in character (cf. Clifford Geertz, Myrdal's Mythology – 'Modernism' and the Third World, *Encounter,* July 1969, XXXIII, No. 1, pp. 26-34). While this may be so, it is at least worth noting that they represent positive values for influential groups in some of the underdeveloped countries and that they were even shared by a man like Gandhi: 'The young Indian must come round to a rational and objective view of material advancement. He must be able and willing to tear himself away from his family ties; flout customs and traditions; put economic welfare before cow worship; think in terms of farm and factory output rather than in terms of gold and silver ornaments; spend on tools and training rather than on temples and ceremonials; work with the low caste rather than starve with the high caste; think of the future rather than of the past; concentrate on material gains rather than dwell on Kismet (destiny). These are extremely difficult changes to envisage in the Hindu social structure and ideas. But they seem unavoidable'. D.K. Rangnekar, *Poverty and Capital Development in India,* London, Oxford University Press, 1958, p. 81, quoted from Myrdal, Asian Drama I, *op. cit.,* p. 62, fn.

possible and desirable states of dynamic balances or processes as goals of social policies and social development. The creative formulation of 'possible and desirable futures' (Ozbekhan) goes far beyond anything that has thus far been undertaken by social analysis. Institutionalists are certainly not the only ones who have something to contribute to these new tasks. They bring to it perhaps a more thorough understanding than other social scientists, of the relevant circular interdependencies which may determine the outcome of action or inaction. My own view is that 'possible and desirable futures' need to be defined with reference not only to general objectives of modernization, but with respect to more specific requirements defined in terms of essential or basic human and collective needs and the minimization of human suffering.

In fact, what is essential, perhaps more than anything else, are new fundamental principles for the determination of social goals and for the formulation of our public policies. Such basic principles must be 'operational', i.e. they must not remain vague and ambiguous like the utilitarian principle of maximizing happiness but must be capable of being translated into criteria of action and into quantifiable indicators of performance. Not maximization of happiness, but the satisfaction of basic human needs or the minimization of human suffering seems to me to constitute such a first principle which could guide practical policies and serve as a yardstick of social efficiency. For, unlike happiness and welfare 'human suffering is utterly concrete ... To wipe out hunger and sickness, unemployment and poverty, illiteracy and ignorance can give rise to practical political action'[33] on a national and international scale. It is this 'inverted utilitarianism' which has been suggested as the first principle which must be our value premise to-day and in the future if we want to come to terms with the problems of environmental and ecological disruption as well as growing national and international disparities, inflation, unemployment, poverty, and last but not least with the threat to world peace.

In this context, I do not consider it as my task to outline the full implications of such a new normative approach to social analysis and social action. Suffice it to say, however, that what would be involved is a basic re-orientation of social analysis which ultimately will have to find

33. Gunnar Adler-Karlsson, Inverted Utilitarianism or a New Way of Life in Developed Countries, Paper presented for the Symposium on a New International Economic Order, The Hague, May 23-24, 1975, ms p. 3.

expression in a reversal of our previous epistemological attitudes and thought processes. Many of the factors which we have so far accepted as given (even if only as parameters) as for example individual preferences, the state of technology, the principle of 'investment at a profit' (as Veblen used to say) will have to be considered as dependent variables which need to be adapted and modified in accordance with the new value premises of minimizing suffering and providing the means for the gratification of basic human needs and the maintenance of essential economic, social and ecological balance.[34]

4.5. Conclusions

I hope to have demonstrated that institutional economists have provided more than a rational critique of the scope and method of traditional economics. They have shown the trans-disciplinary character of our problems, and they have considerably broadened the scope of socio-economic analysis. Above all, they have provided an alternative analytical framework for the explication of the circular interdependencies within a process of cumulative causation which provides economists and other social scientists with a tool for the solution of theoretical and practical problems.

The principle of cumulative causation does not reflect a static view of interdependencies giving rise to a stabilization of the *status quo* within a given form of social organization. The principle does not rule out conflict, tension, contradiction, change, and transformation; on the contrary. Furthermore, the active factors in circular interdependence include both subjective and objective elements: common ideas, valuations, ideologies and institutions as well as techniques, and 'production relations'. While the principle refuses to attribute exclusive or primary

34. For evidence that the practical and political implications of such a re-orientation are being investigated, cf. in addition to Myrdal's writings, Ignacy Sachs, La crise dans les stratégies de développement: Vers l'identification de nouveaux objectifs, OECD, Séminaire: Sciences, Technologie et Développement dans un Monde en Mutation, Paris, 1975. UNEP, The Cocoyac-Declaration, *Development Dialogue,* 1974, No. 2, pp. 88-96. What Now – Another Development, The 1975 Dag Hammarskjöld Report, prepared on the occasion of the 7th Special Session of the United Nations General Assembly. Hasan Ozbekhan, Technology and Man's Future (ms), Santa Barbara 1965. K. William Kapp, Umweltkrise und Nationalökonomie, Schweiz. Ztschr. f. Volksw. und Stat., 108. Jg. Dezember 1972, Heft 3, S. 231-249.

importance to one or the other set of factors in circular interaction, it does not rule out the possibility that either one or the other set of factors may exert a predominant or decisive influence with either positive or negative effects. What the principle rejects as futile is any search for a primary cause.

In this as in other respects, institutionalists have indeed followed the lead of the problems with which they are concerned. This does not preclude specialization nor does it call for expert familiarity of the results of all disciplines. It means, however, as C. Wright Mills put it in another context, that a social scientist will have to be 'familiar enough with the materials and perspectives of other disciplines to use them in clarifying the problems that concern him'.[35] It does not mean that a social scientist needs to master everything and all fields.

The relevant boundaries of the limits of social inquiry differ depending upon the problems under discussion. In any event, in view of the cumulative circular interdependencies which link the economy to the environment and the resource base and hence to the interests of future generations economic processes cannot be adequately described without reference to a time horizon: that is to say, without reference to the time schedule of inputs in relation to scarce available resources, and the direction of the qualitative changes which the use of energy and matter as well as the disposal of waste have upon the environment and hence on economic processes and the well-being of future generations. It is this concern for a longer time horizon and for the complex interdependencies of actual social phenomena and processes moving in a definite direction with possibly irreversible qualitative changes and, last but not least, the rejection and the replacement of the mechanical analogy by the principle of circular causation which gives modern institutionalism, what I venture to call its modern character and its transdisciplinary scope.

35. C. Wright Mills, *Sociological Imagination,* New York, 1959, p. 142.

5. Convergence and diversification in the methodologies of economics and sociology

Ivan Gadourek

5.1. Introduction

A scientific discipline represents a body of knowledge about the related classes of phenomena valid at a given moment of time. It consists of noncontradictory propositions, a part of which, at least, has been corroborated. These definitions imply a dynamic aspect of science. The latter is constantly changing in so far as new propositions are being corroborated or for other reasons added to the system either replacing the old ones or not. What also is implied (by the terms of 'noncontradictory' and 'corroboration') is the fact that the system is changing according to certain rules, established practices and logical norms. The latter are usually referred to by 'method'. Thus we may redefine: science is a body of knowledge arrived at by scientific method.

This emphasis on the methodological aspects of science is necessary where the phenomena studied are familiar to laymen, as is the case with both economics and sociology. Where virtually everbody possesses some knowledge by acquaintance, it is mainly its methodology that justifies the existence of a given scientific discipline.

When considering a possible integration of economics and sociology (or even a merger as some students are inclined to do) it is therefore only too natural to examine the methods of thinking and the ways of working in the two fields. A brief reassessment of what they share in common and what divides them forms the main issue of this paper. An ultimate fusion, a complete annihilation of the boundaries between the two social sciences, is not its direct objective. Even when differences prevail over similarities, a comparison of the methods in the two fields may be fruitful: it helps to uncover the areas of study where sociology and economics ceased to influence each other and where mutual interaction might be promising and desirable, in the future.

A word of caution is in place here. Any student earnestly grappling with the methodological problems of his own discipline will understand how presumptuous it is for a single author to present an over-all comparison of the methods of two sciences. Shortcomings due to the lack of erudition, experience and practice are likely to make themselves felt. Yet, one may ask whether this is not the case with any attempt at interdisciplinary thinking. As the reader will quickly assess, the paper is written by a sociologist whose knowledge of the economists' methods is chiefly of a theoretical nature. His main purpose is to start and ease communication between the two disciplines rather than to pass final judgments on their state of affairs.

Finally, we wish to place the problem in its historical perspective. Economics and sociology have in common such methodology-giants as J.S. Mill, M. Weber and V. Pareto. In the period after the World War I, when the centre of sociological activity moved from France to the United States, a certain estrangement between the two fields took place. While economics reached remarkable achievements in developing macro-theories,[1] sociology (in contradistinction to the standpoint of E. Durkheim) embraced social psychology, dedicated itself to data-gathering rather than theorizing;[2] it became nominalistic in its orientation and focussed on particular 'social problems' rather than on society at large. Some symptoms of the reversal of this trend can be noted,[3] at present. They will be briefly analyzed in this paper.

5.2. Epistemological aspects of economics and sociology

One needs not underwrite all the tenets of positivism to realize that the nature and the choice of a subject co-determines the method of science. A different approach is required in order to ascertain the motives of attempted suicides than to determine the chemical composition of distant

1. See J.M. Keynes, *General Theory of Employment, Interest, and Money*, London, 1936; J.A. Schumpeter, *Capitalism, Socialism, and Democracy*, New York, 1942.
2. John Madge gives a good survey in his *The Origins of Scientific Sociology*, New York, 1962.
3. James S. Coleman, A. Etzioni, and John Porter's *Macrosociology: Research and Theory*, Boston, 1970, may be of a rather programmatic significance. There also appeared H.M. Blalock's *Theory Construction. From Verbal to Mathematical Formulations*, New Jersey, 1969, enabling sociologists to make acquaintance with econometricians' model constructions. Encouraging also are the contributions of the econometricians H. Theil and A.S. Goldberger to sociological reviews and some other initiatives as reviewed in the closing section of this paper.

stars. Those who hesitate to reify the object of their respective science by apriori ascribing some basic traits to it, they also divide science into particular domains, painstakingly confining their own efforts to one of them. Thus implicitly or explicitly scientists delineate their fields and apply a system of classification to sciences. They are, as a rule, very clumsy in doing so, feeling intuitively that they transcend the boundaries of their proper discipline in trying to describe or characterize its subject matter. Several ancient epistemological problems are then fought out in terms of claims one lays upon one's own science: sometimes sophism or the relativity of truth is disguised in the refutation of a value-free science (or, *vice versa*, the belief in the platonic realm of 'ideas' finds its expression in a sharp division of science from valuation), a rationalist belief in innate notions is disguised by a strong emphasis on the formal, logical nature of one's science and its unquestionable findings, while the acceptance of the sensate origin of truth will make a scientist emphasize the empirical nature of his discipline, etc. In the modern scientific frame of reference the problem of epistemology, of the nature of truth and the validity of its cognition, is translated in terms of definition, characterization and classification of science.

The consequences of the latter for the methodology are obvious: it depends on the definition of a scientific domain which problems, which classes of phenomena will be chosen for study. The general characterization of the science, whether it is purely formal or empirical, whether basic or applied, descriptive or explanatory (to mention a few alternatives) will be reflected in the style of work and thought.

The foregoing statement by no means implies that in their actual practice scientists start with definitions and rules of method; often it works the other way round. After years of practice and research, attempts are being made at defining the field and codification of methodological rules. It is our impression that this, exactly, is the way how the science of economics developed. Though there hardly ever was a confusion about its proper subject of study, its formal definition keeps meeting with difficulties until the present day. A presumptuous, all-embracing object ('wealth of nations') has soon been replaced by concepts that laid emphasis on scarcity of commodities or goods. Yet since neither 'scarcity' nor 'goods' are self-evident terms, we get troubles in using them for the purpose of delineating the field of economics from that of related disciplines. For either we take 'scarce goods' as being an economic concept and find ourselves defining economics by terms themselves belonging to the domain and requiring a definition. Or we use 'scarce goods' at its face value and get into difficulties owing to its vague nature. Economists who use the term in their definition are themselves inclined to subsume to it such different objects as services, tenured position and credits. Why not go a step farther? Is power or personal influence not a 'scarce good' in our societies? How then delimitate economics from political science? Is 'blessing' or 'the sacred' not considered as the highest and scarce good by some members of our society? What then, will the boundaries be with religion or the science of religion? We could multiply the instances by focussing our attention on any predominant value (such as 'beauty', 'health', etc.) to find scarcity and raise the question of the distribution of that value over the population.

A general characterization of economics also forms a problem: is it a formal or an empirical science; a basic science or applied; an art? Is it mainly focussed on causal explanation of empirical phenomena or on teleological chains of means and ends? These are still unsettled questions, since consensus has not been reached on them among prominent economists. We should be careful not to dramatize the lack of consensus too much. The situation is not much different with some sister-sciences of *economicis*, as we hope to show presently. And consensus, too, should be measured before we use it as a criterium; a danger of a voluntaristic bias is great in economics and in sociology ('I do not agree with other colleagues thus there is no consensus among them, and their discipline lacks, therefore, scientific status'). Yet, the cleavage between the protagonists of economics as a positive, empirical science, the propositions of which can be tested along the same line as physical or biological hypotheses, and those who consider economics rather as a formal science that assists persons taking economic decisions in a given situation, is not a matter of one single thinker or an insignificant minority alone. It can be traced to the early mental experiments with the idea of an 'economic man', an abstraction representing a supreme rational being that would be guided in his action solely by economic motives and principles. Economics would be nothing more and nothing less than a codification of the principles of action of an 'economic man'. It would be of formal nature, deducing action theorema's from a few axioms in a similar way as geometry deduces her tenets from a few primitive terms. In their opposition to the causal explanation of empirical science some economists of this school embrace teleology as a guiding principle:

economics should order phenomena in chains of ends and means rather than of causes and effects, thus being even more instrumental and subservenient to the man of action. Strangely enough, protagonists of different epistemological doctrines can be found in the teleological school: those who accept Kant's idealism (though they use to add 'critical' to it) and who consider teleology as epistemologically equivalent to causality (these are some thinkers of the 'Austrian school'), logical positivists (e.g. L. von Mises) and historic materialists (e.g. O. Lange, T. Kotarbinski).[4] In so far as they intend to pass logical-normative judgments on how to make rational decisions, these economists are sometimes classified under the 'normative school'. Yet another term coined for theoreticians who take the abstraction of an 'economic man' or person taking optimal rational decisions in a given situation as their starting point is that of 'praxiologists' (derived from 'praxiology' that in Lange's conception pretends to be a logic of practical rational decision-making; I draw on J.J. Klant, 1972).[5]

In contradistinction to the above described school, there are economists who conceive of their discipline as part of general science. They take it for granted that economics can test hypotheses about the optimal production and the distribution of the scarce commodities and goods over a population in a similar objective, universal way as physics or chemistry test their own assumptions and hypotheses.[6] These are the empiricists among the economists (in so far as they emphasize experimental criteria of knowledge), positivists (in so far as they combine formal knowledge with empirical evidence) or operationalists (mainly relying on indicators that link the concepts through the rules of correspondence with the experiential evidence; in an even stricter form: banning the concepts that cannot be thus linked with experiental data out from their theoretical frame-work).

The two main conceptions of economics, the praxiologist and the positivist, if consistently applied, should have major consequences for

4. L. von Mises, *The Ultimate Foundation of Economic Science,* New York, 1962; O. Lange, *Politische Oekonomie,* Vienna 1968; T. Kotarbinski, *Praxiology,* Oxford 1965; for the Austrian school I base myself on the writings of Karel Englis, the first minister of finances of Czechoslovakia.

5. J.J. Klant, *Spelregels voor economen,* Leyden, 1972; also see his article in *De Economist,* 1975, vol. 123, no. 1.

6. M. Friedman, *Essays in Positive Economics,* Chicago, 1953. Also see F. Machlup, 'Operationalism and pure theory in economics' in Sherman R. Krupp (ed.) *The Structure of Economic Science. Essays on Methodology,* Prentice Hall, Englewood Cliffs, N.J. 1966.

the practice of the economic science. When subscribing to the first, an economist builds logically consistent theories that can hardly be refuted empirically ('model platonism') and passes these to the man of practice as a kind of expert adviser thus operating as a master of an applied art rather than a research-worker or a scientist. Operating from the positivist or operationalist standpoint, he will likely be less concerned with the construction of grand theories (that may appear 'empty' i.e. untestable from the empirical point of view), will be more inclined to adjust his theory to the available data and either reject it or use an entire scala of methodological devices to defend it where no direct empirical evidence is available (the methods of 'mental experiment', of 'isolating abstraction', the 'ceteris paribus clause', etc.)

Since its very origin, sociology maintained even closer links with the philosophy of science than did economics. Several of its 'founding fathers' bestowed a good part of their creative thinking on the problem of classification of sciences (A. Comte, J.S. Mill, H. Spencer, in Central Europe: Thomas Masaryk): by consciously launching a new science they tried to make place for it by describing its position with regard to the established scientific disciplines. Like economics, sociology was at first defined by the reference to its global object: society. After one began to realize that existing societies to a certain extent formed quite isolated structures, a shift took place to less all-embracing definitions.

In a tautological way sociology was referred to as the study of social phenomena; fortunately, specifications used to be added to describe the characteristic traits of the class of phenomena under study. Some referred to their origin ('the meaningful social interaction', the social situation where, under a common experience or drive, people co-operate and co-ordinate their activities), others to their basic nature ('the normative constraints of individual behaviour', 'the inner ties binding individuals into groups', etc.). The basic epistemological problem of sociology is also connected with its definitions: the dual nature of social phenomena that are both of a material and of an immaterial nature. For instance, people are often tied together by a religious creed in a sect, or by a political ideology in a party. Since the sects have common meetings, build chapels or wear special clothes, they are visible to observers; so are political gatherings or their consequences: revolutions, wars, coalitions, building projects, etc. Thus the dual nature, symbolic (ideational) and material, characterizes the phenomena that are being studied by sociology.

This has severe consequences for a science that, from its very origin was launched as a positive science, of a general nature, that would study societal phenomena in a similar objective way as does physics approach the phenomena in its own domain. In order to empirically study 'the inner ties that link individuals with a group', these ties had to be made 'visible', available to human perception. This explains why sociologists embraced operationalism willingly; by constructing questionnaires and scales of stimuli they hoped to elicit responses in the subjects that might correspond to responses in real situations. By relying on language as their main source of information (though not the only one: observation of real behaviour and of the real state of affairs also is applied), by resorting to a kind of refined behaviourism that considers verbal behaviour as a specimen of a wider class of behaviour in general, they are faced with severe problems of validation: is covert (verbal) behaviour really equivalent to overt (factual, 'real') behaviour in the field? When administering verbal stimuli to subjects with the intention to make inferences from subjects' differences in reactions to differences in norms and valuations (and similar subjects that sociologists study), what certainty do we have that the stimuli are really all alike? Obviously, the knowledge that all 'questions' were worded in the same way and put in the same sequence is but a poor relief: the *meaning* of words and sentences may differ from individual to individual. It is this inner cleavage between the realm of 'observable' and the realm of 'meanings' that forms the basic epistemological problem of sociology since its early beginning to the present day. The shifting emphasis either from one to another aspect makes for various 'schools' that we may distinguish.

The 'verstehende' sociology finds its continuation in 'phenomenological sociology'; both consider sociology as chiefly an interpretative science. Sociologists of this school try to make the society understandable for its members. The recent trend towards 'ethnomethodological sociology' resembles the foregoing ones, though, as also is the case with the 'symbolic interactionists', somewhat more emphasis is laid on the dynamic nature of the phenomena: one does not limit sociology to the interpretations of social morphology and structure but pays attention to the interpretation of the process of how the social phenomena arise, how they are created and re-created in the daily intercourse between people.[7]

7. H. Garfinkel, *Studies in Ethnomethodology*, Prentice Hall, 1967; A. Schutz, *Collected*

Other sociologists, probably still the main-stream in sociological thought, do not solely confine their discipline to the assessment of meanings, values and norms. They still seek 'external' verification of their hypotheses. They are eventually willing to admit phenomenological (ethnomethodological or semantical) considerations in the first phase of their work while laying stress on the operationalization of concepts and the testing of hypotheses in their actual research. In their conception, sociology is a basic, empirical, generalizing science of social and cultural phenomena. An interesting attempt at synthesis of the two approaches can be found in the 'meaningful-causal method' of Pitirim A. Sorokin.[8] By empathy and also by the simple participation in a cultural system, a sociologist can conceive of hypotheses about why people in a given system behave as they do. He will use careful data-collection and statistical analysis in order to test these hypotheses in an objective way, later on.

After this brief sketch of the epistemological foundations of economics and sociology, an attempt at a comparison can be made. While the main problem of economics seems to be that of reconciling the praxiologist and the positivist views, that of sociology lies in the validation of covert and overt knowledge, in reconciling the interpretative and explanatory conceptions of social science. Both disciplines remain characterized by distinct approaches and fields of study. There hardly can be found an analogy to the 'praxiological' viewpoint, in sociology; 'homo sociologicus', as launched by R. Dahrendorf tries to explain human action entirely by way of social roles.[9] The latter are by no means rational constructs but empirical concepts the content of which varies with each specific social structure (nation, institution, cultural era or area). Some rational theories of 'adaptive behaviour' (E. Wight Bakke) usually lack any predictive value since the concepts used are not measureable, are not rooted in social reality by means of fixed rules of correspondence. *Ex post* one always can argue that an Actor (an imaginary agent in the field) was motivated by the pursuit of pleasure or of recompense: even to

Papers I and II, The Hague, 1962 and 1964; A.V. Cicourel, *Cognitive Sociology, Language and Meaning in Social Interaction,* London, Penguin 1973.

8. This proved, however, not very fruitful in research practice; no example of application is known to me. For its description see Pitirim A. Sorokin, *Society, Culture, and Personality,* Harper & Brothers, 1947.

9. R. Dahrendorf, *Homo Sociologicus,* Westdeutscher Verlag, Köln u. Opladen, 1960.

martyrs one may ascribe masochistic motives or an identification with the imaginary community of saints. *A priori* the assumption that 'every human being acts in pursuit of pleasure or of social recompense' lacks any explanatory, any praxiological or teleological value, since virtually any act can be subsumed under 'pleasure' or 'social recompense', even acts contradicting each other ('the henchman' vs. 'the martyr' in the foregoing example).

While there is hardly any successful theory of 'social rationality' in sociology that would resemble that of an 'economic man', there is hardly any questioning of the validity of economic concepts and data in *economicis* either. Relying on the solid book-keeping of countless instances (firms, bureau's of revenues and taxes, banks, etc.), economists do not endure critical attacks as sociologists do who have to account for the distortion of reality owing to the limitations of language, owing to the tendency of people to give socially desirable answers, to evade threatening questions, to forget traumatic experiences, etc. etc. Instead, they go on with their theory-construction; for them, methodology is still the way of logical theory-building, a codification of rules to which economic or econometrist theory-building should conform.[10]

If we, tentatively, conclude that as far as their fields and epistemological nature are concerned, economics and sociology still form distinct sciences, is there, in this respect, nothing they can teach each other? There might be some lessons to learn. Since sociology studies such categories as culture-pattern, social structure and social order, it may draw the attention of some economists to the fields bordering on their own discipline and help to define more sharply their study-object. For sociologists, economic institutions exist side by side with the political, religious, recreational, educational and other institutions. Several of these gave rise to specialized social or human sciences: science of politics, of education, even of religion (differing from theology which is usually linked with the teaching of a particular church). As we already mentioned above, economists should try to delineate their field with regard to each of these, especially, political science. As far as sociology is concerned, it resembles in this context rather an 'open system', crossing the border-lines between the specialized human and social sciences, and studying *external* relationships between the social pheno-

10. The subtitle of the Dutch book of Klant (see note 5) sounds: 'The logical structure of economic theories' (my translation).

mena in the first place, thus not meddling with the phenomena *within* the differentiated systems themselves. An economic sociologist might thus study the impact of religious doctrine on the economic Actor or the political consequences of an economic action (the latter only if politicologists ignore them); he hardly feels justified to formulate the laws or relationships within the proper domain of economic activity. It would be just as absurd to study the uniformities in economic behaviour without the knowledge of economics, as it is absurd for a sociologist to study uniformities in surgeons' proper conduct without the knowledge of pathological anatomy. Naturally, sociology may shed some light upon the intriguing problem of how different systems (family-relationships, social classes or castes, religious beliefs or practices, etc.) encroach upon the economic system, how the family-man, the political man (and not to forget: the idle man, pursuing recreational activities) compete with the economic man.

In turn, sociology will learn from economists that it is probably a futile expectation to try to find rational theories of human conduct in general, unless we resort to special sciences or to domains of rational decision making, not yet covered by specialized science. As a matter of fact, there is no science nor a theoretical model of the ways people spend their leisure, though the choice between various alternative leisure activities (or: states of mind) strongly resembles consumers' preferences for goods, and time bestowed can be quantified as easily as money. No wonder that many sociologists are working on it; yet difficulties here will probably be greater rather than lesser when compared with the models of utility functions extant[11]. For the rest they will have to abide by the common social rules that guide the conduct of chessmen as well as of those e.g. attending religious rituals; but these rules will hardly result in closely knit theories from which fruitful empirical hypotheses can be derived.

11. See, for instance, R. Wippler, 'Private and public models of spending leisure time and their relevance for ecological problems'; a Paper Presented at the Third Biennial Conference of the International Society for the Study of Behavioral Development, University of Surrey, Guilford, July 13-17, 1975.

5.3. Some lexical aspects of economists' and sociologists' frames of reference

The nature of phenomena that a particular science studies and the basic characterization of that particular science make for the more specific aspects of scientific methodology. Its more general aspects are due to the mutual contact between scientists or to the methodology of science. From the latter, one borrows the basic categories that influence not only the way of thinking but also the decision on whether data and what data should be collected, and in what way they should be processed. 'Description', 'classification', 'causal explanation', 'structural relationship', 'teleology', – these are but a few examples of the categories in question. They usually spread from one discipline to another (think of 'structure' !), their impact varies with time: after a time of frequent use and popularity, times of temporal or permanent decline set in. Their acceptance or refutation only partly depends on immanent considerations (as based on the development of the science itself); for a larger part it is dictated by the philosophy of science at that moment and, perhaps – by fashion. It is a merit of Kuhn that he opened the discussion of the external causes of what he calls the changing 'paradigms' in science.[12]

It would take us too far to give a minute analysis of the use of various categories by the two sciences; it would require careful classification and a lot of counting of the major contributions to either discipline (e.g. content analysis of articles in the leading journals). Instead, a somewhat impressionistic sketch will be given.

Though many will hesitate to recognize it as a basic category, 'description' should be treated in the first place. Important periods of science, several branches of contemporary science (botany, zoology, crystallography, etc.) are characterized by detailed description of carefully observed facts. Some historians of science are inclined to think that 'description' characterizes an early stage of development of a science that tends to 'explanation' in its more mature phases. Others ignore the distinction altogether revoking Newton's reference to his law of gravitation as 'a concise description' of the state of the world. It is, of course, a description of collected facts in rather non-scientific terms that concerns us here.

It still flourishes in sociology. Though the time of descriptive

12. T.S. Kuhn, *The Structure of Scientific Revolutions*, Chicago, 1962.

community studies seems to be over by now (even in the Netherlands where 'sociography' used to be a recognized discipline), description of structures, processes and even states of mind abound in sociological literature: hospitals described as specimens of caste-society, the rôle enactment problems of a bisexual Agnes after a surgical operation, experiences of a marihuana smoker, etc. etc. In studies leaning towards the cultural anthropological tradition 'description' is an even more dominant category.

In economics, according to my impression, 'description' plays a much more subordinate rôle. It can still be found in some marginal fields of institutional economics and of business economics. Moreover, it is often confined to one or a few parameters; one 'describes' e.g. the income distribution of employers in a given year in a given country, the demand for cash money in a given period of time, etc. In the latter case, one resorts to technical terms or the apparatus of descriptive statistics, operating on a higher level of abstraction that hardly justifies the term 'description'. In this field, moreover, a convergence takes place, since sociology also attempts to ascertain some parameters such as the consumption of medicines and of medical services, the satisfaction with housing conditions, the preference for a certain political system, etc., etc. Yet, leaving these exceptions aside, explanation prevails over description in economics while this hardly can be said with any certainty for sociology.

As far as 'classification' is concerned, the situation is quite similar. It was John Madge who propagated the term of 'taxonomic definition' in sociology: one classifies societal phenomena in a similar way as botany used to classify plants, by building entire systems of species and kinds, and by delineating the generic and the more specific properties of the subjects under study, handling cabbages and kings basically alike, to speak with Alice in Wonderland. Taxonomy governs not only the process of ordering the data (dividing, for instance, all interviewees into low-grade or high-grade educational classes, or into one of the six socio-economic-status classes) but penetrates the process of theory-formation.[13] A good part of what passes for theory in sociology consists, in fact, of classificatory schemata, sometimes of a typological nature. This holds for practically all the great theoreticians, whether we take

13. R. Wippler, 'Theorie, taxonomie en model in de sociologie' (Theory, taxonomy and model in sociology) in *Mens en Maatschappij*, Jrg. 44, no. 4, 1969.

Pitirim A. Sorokin, his great opponent in Harvard, Talcott Parsons, or Robert K. Merton who took a somewhat mediate position. Three basic types of culture, four 'pattern variables', five 'models of individual adaptation' – it is interesting to note that exhaustive typologies are being built. A variety of cultural patterns is pressed into three basic types, an even larger variety of ways individuals function in a societal setting is confined to five (no more and no less) types. No wonder that students of economics who take sociology as their minor subject complain of a necessity to train their memorizing again in order to learn all the new names sociology has to offer them: words, words.

The confrontation is striking, since the core of economic theory formation is analytical. To revoke the term coined by the psychologist Kurt Lewin, the mode of thinking of an economist is prevalently Galilean, while sociology still sticks with to an Aristotelian pattern of thinking. Economics seeks the mechanisms that would explain the processes of change in the dynamic field of economic variables while sociology, to a good deal, is preoccupied with describing the 'substances' and classifying them in their 'natural' classes. Seen against this background, the theoretical work of George C. Homans and Peter M. Blau (to say nothing of protagonists of mathematical sociology, such as James C. Coleman and some younger Dutch theoreticians) signifies an innovatory trend.[14]

Practically absent in economics are some categories that sociology owes to the humanities, owing to her dual nature that was referred to above. A good example is the operation called 'Verstehen', i.e. interpretation of the cultural meanings that characterize social behaviour ('hermeneutics' is another term that we come across in the writings of some European thinkers; one tries to interpret or reconstruct the meaning from the context in which a sign or a symbol occurs, in a similar way as religious books used to be interpreted by careful contextual scrutiny).[15] 'Interpretation' in general, though rather its connotation of 'ascribing cultural meaning' than 'ascribing individual's motives of action', is often used in sociological theory.

14. George C. Homans, *Social Behavior: Its Elementary Forms,* New York, 1961; Peter M. Blau, *Exchange and Power in Social Life,* New York, 1964; H. Turk & R.L. Simpson, (Ed.), *Institutions and Social Exchange: the Sociologies of Talcott Parsons and George C. Homans,* New York, 1971. James S. Coleman, *Introduction to Mathematical Sociology,* The Free Press of Glancoe, 1964.

15. See *Hermeneutik und Dialektik, Festschrift für H.G. Gadamer,* Tübingen, 1970. G. Radnitzky, *Contemporary Schools of Metascience,* II, Göteborg, 1970.

This does not mean that 'explanation' or 'prediction', are absent from today-sociology. In discussions about its methodological problems they are, according to my impression, even more frequently used than in economic literature; in the latter, actually more explanatory models and explanations are presented. There seems to be a certain paradox here: a science that actually successfully applies them, does not frequently explicitly mention the categories of explanation, while a science for which the application is still problematical, abounds in treatises on 'causal explanation'. Alike 'explanation', 'causation' and 'causality' are employed in both sciences. The same fluctuation of the popularity of the concept can be noticed in either discipline. While very much used in the nineteenth century, 'causality' was looked upon with mistrust in the period between the two wars when alternative subcategories have been launched to substitute the concept which was undermined by the thinking about indeterminism and relativity: independent and dependent variables, pluri- or multicausality, etc. H.A. Simon's seminal article on spurious correlation (*J.A.S.A.* 1954) was accepted both by economists (econometricians) and sociologists and helped to draw causality back from oblivion and restore its value as an explanatory concept.

As to 'teleology', it hardly was used by sociologists at all, while now and then being referred to in economic literature (L. von Mises, Adolph Lowe) either explicitly or implicitly in terms of goals-and-means instrumentalism.[16]

Another category dividing the two disciplines is that of 'model' which is employed much more often and with a different connotation in economics than in sociology. While a good part of contemporary econometrics consists of models of various degrees of complexity, models are utterly scarce in sociology, and if available, of an utmost simple nature (usually networks of linear relationships connecting some four or five variables measured imperfectly, on ordinal level at the best). Moreover, sociological models are thought to be testable, while some economists consider the purely formal, deductive nature of a model, as a feature that distinguishes it from a testable theory.

There also are differences in the way the category of 'structure' is used. While in economics it is of a purely formal nature, designating a system of causal relationships (without exclusion of reciprocal relations),

16. R.L. Heilbroner (Ed.) *Economic Means and Social Ends. Essays in Political Economics*, Prentice Hall, 1969.

in sociology it often is either reified or vested with material, experiential contents; social structure designates a pattern of social positions that are occupied by Actors of varying social status, performing more or less institutionalized acts, the social roles. Though 'structure' in its formal connotation (launched, if I am not mistaken, by Vilfredo Pareto) is also used by sociologists, it is this concrete concept of structure that is quite typical of sociology and cannot be transferred to other sciences because of its specific nature.

Another category, often used by sociologists, is practically absent in economics: that of 'function'. To specify: 'function' in the meaning in which it is used by functional sociologists, is unknown to economists. Sociologists resort to this category to describe the consequences of a social institution for other institutions or the society as a whole – once more it is vested with concrete meaning. These consequences can be consciously pursued and known (a manifest function) or they may be unknown (latent function) or even unwanted (dysfunction). Obviously, neither the mathematical function of an econometrician, nor the task-field of an executive in an enterprise that a business-economist tries to describe by his category of 'function', covers the connotations of the sociologist's category. (On purpose, we use 'function' without reference to the adjustment of the social system or of a society as a whole that some sociologists use and which makes the cleavage between the two concepts even larger). There has been some futile controversy between sociologists and business economists in the Netherlands, based on the semantic confusion about the category of 'function'.[17]

Yet, here we already leave the categories of the general methodology, without having exhausted its entire field. We could have enlarged on some of them, but the enterprise looks unrewarding. Both sociology and economics use 'induction' as well as 'deduction' but the emphases are different. In spite of applying Popper's methodology, sociology remains overwhelmingly an inductive science, economics a deductive one. Realizing what has been said about the categories of 'model', 'description' and 'classification', this will not astonish us too much.

Summing up this section, we may state that in terms of the categories of their basic frames of reference, sociology and economics once more appear as two distinct disciplines. Description, taxonomy and various forms of interpretation of meaning (hermeneutics) are comparatively

17. J.A.A. van Doorn, *Sociologie van de organisatie*, Leiden, 1956.

unknown to economists while still playing an important part in sociology. In turn, economics applies teleology, thinking in terms of ends and means (instrumentalism) which is almost entirely unknown in sociology; it also builds formal, deductive models of reality which are only sporadically found in sociology. Some categories are used with different connotations: structure is usually *formally* defined in economics (a manifold of related positions) and *substantially,* in sociology; and function, which is either used in its mathematical or business connotation by economists while maintaining a specific meaning for sociology (where it leans back on biology, especially physiology).

Can the two disciplines influence each other in this field, by exchanging the basic categories of their frames of references? It is enticing to think that some branches of economic activity (e.g. institutional economics) might profit by applying the functional analysis of sociologists. Yet a question arises: will it still be economics, that issues? If attention is paid to other than economic functions, one transcends the field of economics and carries out sociological analysis. If economic functions (for instance, of the central bank in the national economies in a number of developed countries) are studied, will the concept enrich existing knowledge? Is it meaningful to speak of latent and manifest economic functions or of economic dysfunctions? There may be some doubts. But there is little doubt about the usefulness of the general institutional-functional approach, as any student in the Netherlands will ascertain when trying to answer such elementary questions as: what (social) action is needed to raise the price of milk by one cent? or – for that matter – the wages of semiskilled workers? Sociology, in its turn, surely might profit by embracing instrumentalism, teleology or praxiology. By learning systematically to seek sociological means to achieve useful goals, the present strategy of *ad hoc* investigations might be abandoned and by focussing on more distant goals more socially relevant knowledge might be achieved. Yet even this statement might be no more than wishful thinking; it should be subjected to testing.

We are on more solid grounds when pleading for semantic caution with regard to the overlapping categories. Time consuming discussions can be avoided when one realizes that 'structure' is not necessarily 'social stucture' in the two sister social sciences and that 'function' might have a different connotation in two disciplines even though both employ mathematics, logic and the tools of statistics.

5.4. The nature of problems and the design of studies

The way in which certain problems are chosen as subjects for investigation, is one of the neglected domains of scientific enquiry. Yet, ever since Max Scheler, we realize its importance, since it is here where external factors enter the scientific discipline, either hampering or promoting the development of science. Since the choice of a problem often functions as a guideline for further investigations, helping the scientist to design his study in order to find a satisfactory answer, we decided to treat problem-raising and study-design in the two sciences together.

It would be interesting to analyze doctoral dissertations in the two disciplines in this respect, in order to approach the subject in a more objective way. By lack of time, only some hypothetical statements will be launched here.

With all due caution then, there seem to be differences in the way of asking the questions. Sociologists imitate the style of other behavioural scientists in directly questioning the 'state of nature': does the blood of the productive scientists contain more uremic acid than the blood of less productive scientists? does the Roman Catholic part of the population generally display more optimistic attitudes than the Calvinist segment of the population? do overwhelmingly secular communities display tendencies to political radicalization? There are hardly any essential differences between the first question (asked by a physiologist) and the sociologists' questions. They directly lead to data collection and can be answered with comparatively little thinking but considerable effort: one does one's own data collection, often draws a cross-sectional sample of a total population and questions thousands of people in order to solve one's problem.

Economists rather resemble scholars than research-workers in their style of work. Overlooking the data that have been collected for them by the central planning bureaus, by the bureau of census or other authorities, looking at the balance-sheets or organization-charters of their enterprises they often perform a kind of mental experiment: 'just imagine that ...' or 'let's pretend that ...' ('our country would overnight disarm; what would be the economic consequences of the deed? if we regard an enterprise as a system in the meaning which system-theory ascribes to it, what would (should) the economic and/or organizational consequences be?'). To answer this kind of questions, economists usually do a lot of thinking, trying to deduce the consequences which the imaginary state of affairs would have for their models of reality, remodelling this reality, and only occasionally confronting the newly built model with facts. The latter are, as a rule, once more the ready-made data of accountants or of officials of planning bureaus, 'secondary data' in terms of data collection research.

One hardly can overestimate the importance of the availability of data for economists. This probably explains why they usually operate on a macro- or maeso-level, while most sociologists address individual interviewees to collect their data, even when studying firms. The economic conduct of firms can be deduced from the collectively drawn balance-sheets; the satisfaction of employees, their feeling of well-being or attachment to the firm can only be assessed by means of interviews with individuals. Only in the marginal fields of economics (the study of consumers' behaviour), does some micro-analysis take place. Yet, here again a question can be asked: is it still economics or psychology c.q. sociology that empirically studies consumers' choice? Hand in hand with opting for a certain level of analysis goes the actual design of the data collection process. While economists shrug their shoulders when hearing that their sociological colleague chose for active participation in a drug-scene in order to learn the norms and habits governing its functioning, or launched a scouting expedition into the households of Argentinean workers trying to assess the prevailing anticonceptual practices there, their own work will be frowned upon by sociologists as being based on secondary data *only*, not containing any *original* materials.

Out of the many testing devices common in sociology, but a few have been taken over by economists. Especially striking is the absence of experimental thinking in economics. Both sciences are faced with ethical and factual difficulties in artificially manipulating the variables in their theories or models. Yet, not all variables are existentially determined (to the extent 'sex', 'religious denomination' or 'age' are so for a sociologist) and are open to experimental manipulation. Successful experiments have been carried out with the exposure to mass-media, to training courses or treatment in the field of health. Comparatively few experiments are being done with organizational factors, with various forms of financial incentive. Moreover, designs such as evaluation-research (trying to ascertain empirically the consequences of certain changes) are seldom planned by economists. Neither is 'action research' recommended to ministers of finances by their economic colleagues (if they are not, perchance, economists themselves). Some quasi-experimental designs, as the ex-post-facto studies based on matched variables, are practically unknown to economists. On the other hand, the latter were very quick in discovering the value of a computer for simulation. Yet, paradoxically enough, the large part of computer similation projects is concerned with model-simulation rather than with the simulation of economic processes as based on empirically measured parameters. What are the reasons for this relative neglect of pseudo- or semi-experimental methods? According to my impression, the mighty tool of parametric statistical analysis should be mentioned in the first place. Thanks to the fact that the basic variables in economic models are quantified on ratio or interval levels of measurement, the fine tools of mathematical calculus and of multivariate analysis can be applied substituting statistical control of interfering variables for experimental controls. This brings us, however, to the next section of this paper.

Summing up, we wish to point out that economists differ from sociologists in the kind of questions they ask (of a more conditional nature), in their emphasis on macro- and maeso-analysis, in their employment of ready-made data, calculus, computer-simulation and multivariate-analysis. Sociologists were characterized as still being data-collectors more frequently than economists, as submitting simpler hypotheses to direct empirical tests in various semi-experimental designs or designs aimed at primary data collection. The work-style of the latter resembles that of research-workers in some biological sciences, while economists' work can perhaps be placed somewhere between that of a scholar and of a statistical or mathematical analyst.

The possibility to learn from each other has already been stipulated above. Considering the large quantity of data that have been collected by various institutes for public opinion research and by other research-institutes, the development of a socially relevant macro-sociology seems both desirable and feasible. Computer simulation could also be applied to domains other than demography or voting behaviour only, as economic simulation distinctly shows. Business economists could take over some experimental designs to evaluate measures they take (or advise), macro-economists also could build in pieces of evaluation-research, to follow up the appropriateness of their models and their decision making. Either of them will have accomodated qualitative, 'sociological and psychological', variables into their models and have drawn methodological consequences from it, by then.

5.5. Collection and analysis of data

Nowhere, probably, are the tendencies towards the diversification of sociology and economics more striking than in their methods of handling the data. Roughly a generation ago, in the period after the WW II, economics, sociology, and psychology each pursued its distinct, own way.

Economics was under the spell of econometrics that was established as a new discipline in the years immediately preceding the war. It applied sophisticated models of analysis of systems of linear, simultaneous equations embracing few quantitative variables. The data for analysis were chiefly of an aggregate nature, pertaining to the economy of a country (e.g. the United States) in a series of successive years. Though the term 'measurement' was often explicitly used, it usually referred to derived measures based on the same aggregate data on which other variables were based. Attempts to measure, for instance, 'the propensity to consume' or 'the demand for food' directly, by collecting appropriate data from a probabilistic sample of a population had to wait until George Katona started his work at Ann Arbor in the early fifties. The solution of the problem of identification of a system of structural equations, going hand in hand with the use of multiple regression techniques of analysis, resulted in several prediction studies. These, however, were not always applied in order to test the adequacy of the model; rather they were used as forecasts or 'numerical illustrations' of the models extant. The low multiple correlations were 'explained' by referring to the deficiencies of the structural models in this respect, when compared with purely empirical, statistical procedures. The latter seek to maximize coefficients by the selection of optimal predictors *ex post,* while structural relations are *apriori* determined.

While economics and/or econometrics, in order to saveguard the identifiability of their models, confined themselves to self-contained systems of a limited number of variables, psychology took rather an opposite stand in this respect. Thanks to the progress of test-construction and measurement as pioneered by Thurstone and Likert, countless scales have been devised to measure the 'vectors of mind', personality traits and attitudes. To bring some order into the gamut of partial results of measurement, psychologists started to treat the testscores as representing quantitative variables and to analyze them accordingly by applying parametric statistics.

Factor analyses of various kinds have been applied to matrices of raw scores or of correlations, in order to reduce the data to a manageable number of 'general traits', 'basic attitudes' or in what other manner the resulting factors have been referred to. Frequently, existential factors (sex, age, socio-economic status or educational level, etc.) have also been added. Thus large matrices were analyzed and multi-variate techniques were applied to what definitely may be regarded as underidentified systems at present. While econometrics neglected measurement in the proper sense, 'a theory of data' and the 'theory and methods of scaling' have been launched by psychologists, thus laying the foundations for a theory of measurement.

While considerable achievements have been attained by econometricians in the field of solving systems of simultaneous or structural equations psychologists were no less inventive in improving their factor-analytical tools, that became largely standardized and led to invariant, mathematically founded results. Moreover, other multivariate techniques of both exploratory and confirmatory nature have been developed and successfully applied to psychological data: cannonical correlation, discriminant analysis, etc.

Sociologists took an in-between position. Thanks to Lazarsfeld and Guttman, early attempts have been made to measure the by origin qualitative properties. Especially scales of Guttman-type, requiring little mathematical insight, were embraced by sociologists immediately after the fourth volume of the *American Soldier* appeared, in 1950.[18] The development of homogeneous scales of ordinal-level of measurement went hand in hand with an equally rapid development of nonparametric statistics. This, together with the already mentioned preference for work at micro-level of analysis and for primary data collection, made for a closed research-structure that replaced the correlational macro-analysis of the period between the wars.

In this situation, considerable changes took place recently. Some distinct signs of convergence and integration are noticeable in each of the three disciplines. In economics, more attention is given to qualitative variables that used to be excluded from the models, up to now. In 1971, just 21 years after Cyril Burt published his treatise on the factor analysis of qualitative data, a Dutch econometrician, M.A. Kooyman, published his study on the use of dummy variables in econometrics, chiefly in

18. S.A. Stouffer et al., *Measurement and Prediction,* Princeton U. Press, 1950.

regressionmodels. Burt himself used dummies together with tetrachoric r's to which he applied factor analysis, using both dichotomies and polytomies.[19] One year before the appearance of Kooyman's dissertation Richard P. Boyle published an article on 'Path analysis and ordinal data' in the January-issue of the *American Journal of Sociology* (1970) in which he advocated the use of dummies in the path-analytical studies that became very popular with sociologists towards the end of 'sixties (see below). His article met with many reactions from his colleagues and from statisticians in sociological journals.

Other attempts at coping with qualitative data are made, one of which deserves our attention. Henri Theil, an econometrician, published an extensive treatment of four sociological examples by means of a 'logit-analysis' in the same journal of sociology (July, 1970). In his 'Estimation of Relationships Involving Qualitative Variables', Theil presents methods of estimating linear logit relations between four or more polytomies or dichotomies, with or without interaction, thus proposing a qualitative analogy to the multiple-regression, and going even beyond the latter in estimating the effects in the quasi-experimental designs.

Again, there are convergent trends in sociology. Of decisive influence was, probably, the publicity given to H.A. Simon's method of isolating spurious from genuine correlations (by partializing) by H.M. Blalock, the author of a widely used statistics textbook for sociologists. Blalock extended Simon's model to include more than three variables; later on, he embraced path-analysis and also published a book on *Theory Construction; From Verbal to Mathematical Formulation* (Prentice Hall, 1969) paraphrasing some recent econometrist literature in a very popular way for the use by sociologists. While the dynamic models which he described met with but little response until now (perhaps owing to the mathematical prerequisites, the knowledge of the calculus), 'path-analysis' or its modified version, Boudon's 'dependence analysis' became extremely popular with sociological research-workers. After having applied Guttman scaling or factor-analysis to their items in order to reduce their data, they often present their results in the form of a recursive system of equations, solved by successively replacing the correlations found by the path- or dependence coefficients denoting the

19. Cyril Burt, 'The factorial analysis of qualitative data', In the *British J. of Psychology, Statistical Section,* III, 1950, pp. 166-185.
M.A. Kooyman, *Onechte variabelen in de ekonometrie,* Assen, 1971.

strength of causal influences. Economists would find the error-terms exasperatingly high (the correlation of alienation, $\sqrt{1-R^2}$, often amounting to values between .75 en .85), yet one has to bear in mind that individual persons' responses, that are submitted to high variation, formed the basis of the data. Several devices (e.g. the correlation of attenuation) have been used to boost the results. The limitation of such models lies in the tediousness of the work: it costs a lot of work to solve the system of equations pertaining to some seven or nine variables by the usual method of substitution on which Boudon's methodology is based. Peculiarly, it was the econometrician A.S. Goldberger[20] who drew the attention to the fact that Boudon's dependence analysis is, in fact, but a modification of multiple regression analysis. Accordingly, computer programs can, with success, be applied to solve the more intricate systems of equations, as we learned from our own experience. It is typical of the present interaction of the two disciplines in this field, that Goldberger published his review in a sociological journal. Together with the sociologist Otis Dudley Duncan, he edited *Structural Equation Models in the Social Sciences* (Seminar Press, New York, London, 1973) in which sociologists and econometricians intermingle with psychologists.

The contribution of the latter should not be underestimated. Almost similtaneously with Goldberger, a Dutch mathematical psychologist J.P. van der Geer, has shown how to solve the complex path-analytical models by resorting to the square root method which he considers as one of the many variants of factor analysis. As we know, in matrix formulation the beta-coefficients can be derived from the inverted correlation matrix of the predictor-variable post-multiplied by the vector of the correlations of the dependent variable with the predictors:

$$\beta = \mathbf{R}_{pp}^{-1}\mathbf{r}_{pc} \; .$$

Thus any method of matrix-inversion will do to obtain the beta's. By setting the non-significant beta's equal to zero and readjusting the remaining beta's, exactly the same results issue as when Boudon's dependence analysis is used in the cases where structural models fit the data. Again the use of computers that often either deliver beta-

20. See Goldberger's review in *American Sociological Review*, 1970, Vol. 35: 97-101; 'On Boudon's Method of Linear Causal Analysis.'

coeficients directly or contain the matrix-inversion (of a large number of variables) as a sub-routine, suggests itself.

Another finding in Van der Geer's *Introduction to Multivariate Analysis* (W. Freeman & C., San Francisco, 1971) is the basic functional unity that exists between Tj. Koopman's method of weighted regression analysis and the canonical factor analysis thus making multivariate-analysis a suitable tool for the determination of the elasticity coefficients.

Long before Van der Geer, A. Mol (Groningen University) advocated the application of factor-analysis to economic models by letting the rotation-axes coincide with the main independent (exogeneous) variables (a rotation called 'caumax'-method, supposed to maximize the causal interpretation).[21] In an article on 'Econometrics and psychometrics: a survey of communalities' (*Psychometrika,* June, 1971) Arthur S. Goldberger also states a gap between the two disciplines. He, however, mentions that Koopmans and Reirsøl pointed at the close connection between identification in simultaneous equation models and in factor analysis models as early as 1950. Goldberger himself refers to M. Friedman's 'permanent income model' and to Keynes' 'aggregate demand model' to show that econometrics, at present, also deals with unobserved variables; 'permanent income', in terms of test score theory, appears as the *true score* while measured income and measured consumption are *congeneric tests.*

Returning to sociology, we may point to the fact that Henry Theil's logit analysis in its modified form, as elaborated by the mathematical statistician-sociologist Leo Goodman and warmly advocated and propagated by James A. Davis, both from the University of Chicago, have been accepted by American sociologists.[22] From econometrics they have taken over the habit to view time as a variable and employ it in 'log-linear cohorte analyses of social change'. Instead of panel data, the data of two

21. Th.J. Ferrari, J. Mol, 'Factor analysis of causal models', in *Netherlands' Journal of Agricultural Sciences,* 1967, 15, pp. 38-49. J. Mol, 'De economische onderzoeker en zijn ruimte', *Maandschrift Economie,* 1966, XXX, pp. 367-376.

22. See Leo A. Goodman, 'A modified multiple regression approach to the analysis of dichotomous variables', *American Sociological Review,* 1972, Vol. 37: 28-46; *id.:* 'Causal analysis of data from panel studies and other kinds of surveys' *in American J. of Sociology,* 1973, Vol. 78: 1135-1191; *id.:* 'The analysis of systems of qualitative variables when some variables are unobservable. Part I: a modified latent structure approach', in *American J. of Sociology,* 1974 Vol. 79: 1179-1259.
James A. Davis, 'Hierarchical models for significance tests in multivariate contingency tables: An exegesis of Goodman's recent papers', in H.L. Costner (ed.) *Sociological Methodology 1974,* Jossey-Bass Inc., San Francisco, London, 1974.

subsequent cross-sectional surveys employing identical questions, are used. Goodman-models take the logarithms of odds as a basis for the calculation of 'effects', either of direct effects of independent variables or their combinations (interactions). Goodman recently expanded his hierarchical models to cover polytomies as well as dichotomies and wrote a computer programme for the likelihood ratio chi-square values and goodness-of-fit chi-square statistics for any of the numerous unsaturated models obtained by setting some of the beta's equal to zero.

Goodman published more than 150 pages in the two leading American journals of sociology, expounding his method; he maintains that it is applicable to observed as well as unobserved variables, to survey-data as well as to panel data (collected at two or more moments of time). The fact remains that interaction between economists and sociologists in this field is very intensive, at present; an important role (as mediator) has been played by the mathematical statistician, the usual selfless promotor of science.

We do not wish to idealize the situation too much. Editing books together, reviewing each other's work, taking over each other's techniques in some fields does not imply that all differences in the approach to data have disappeared between economists and the behavioural scientists. The field of measurement still forms a stumbling block between the disciplines. Where psychometrics developed an entire scale of techniques on how to assess the reliability of data and launched several concepts of validity (face-validity, construct-validity, correlational validity, etc.), sociologists somehow neglect them in their recent work. One of the reasons may be the resort to homogeneous scales. Guttman's and Loevinger's scales implied internal consistency (on which earlier split-half techniques of assessment of reliability were based). Though not explicitly mentioned by the constructors of scales, validity measures are made available in studies especially designed for this purpose.[23] Moreover, the comparatively recently accepted path-analytical models give a double *impetus* to revived interest in reliability. For instance, A. Stinchcombe suggested[24] to use communalities from factor-analytical studies as possible estimators of reliabilities and to use

23. Seymour Sudman & Norman M. Bradburg, *Response Effects in Surveys. A Review and Synthesis*, Aldine Publishing Co., Chicago, 1974.

24. Arthur L. Stinchcombe, 'A heuristic procedure for interpreting factor analysis' in *Amer. Sociol. Review*, 1971, Vol. 36: 1080-1084.

the latter in correlations of attenuations in regressionmodels, thus boosting the beta-weights. Siegel and Hodge, on the other hand, use path-analysis to assess the internal structure of scales and indexes by using causal paths instead of correlations in the usual forms of item-analysis.[25]

Econometricians might consider errors in their stochastic equations, yet these are usually treated as imponderabilia, subjected to many assumptions (e.g. independance of exogeneous terms), now and then admitted to be violated when the model does not fit the data. The data are seldom an object of scrutiny, one does not examine the internal structure of various indices used. This remark may sound rather heretic in Groningen where F. de Jong and H. de Haan launched the dimensional analysis of economic data.[26] But we should bear in mind, that this approach is based on ratio-measures, thus probably at the very opposite end of the scale of quantification as sociology that chiefly operates with ordinal scales. This intern confinement of dimensional analysis to variables that have been measured on ratio-level imposes limits on economic models themselves, for only economic variables in the narrowest sense, measureable in money, can be included in the models and systems of equations that are required to be homogeneous in the dimensional analysis sense (the Pi-theorema of Fourrier and Buckingham).

Hand in hand with the problem of measurement goes the treatment of aggregate data. For economists operating with the data of central authorities the main import is that of disaggregation: when comparing various indices for different countries a question of validity arises.

Do the index-figures measure the same quantities? The need for standardization of measures boils down to a necessary decomposition of the macro-economic indices. Even then the problem is not solved yet: we may derive measures for "the propensity to consume', or 'the demand for food' exclusively from macro-economic indices as disposable income per capita, food consumption per capita, retail prices of food

25. Paul M. Siegel, Robert W. Hodge, 'A causal approach to the study of measurement error' in H.M. Blalock and Ann B. Blalock, (ed.), *Methodology in Social Research,* McGraw Hill, 1971.

26. F.J. de Jong, *Dimensional Analysis for Economists,* Amsterdam, 1967, H. de Haan, *De toepassing van de dimensieanalyse op de econometrie,* Katholieke Universiteit, Leuven (Belgium), 1970 (mimeographed). D.H. Krantz et al. *Foundations of Measurement,* Academic Press, New York, London, 1971, Chapter 10.

products, etc. It is, however, the individual consumer who is either willing to spend or to save, either spending more money on food or on durables.

Under which conditions of presuppositions are we allowed to infer from structural or statistical associations between macro-economic dimensions to regularities governing individual conduct? Quite a lot of work has been done to solve this problem. The solution coincides probably, though only in part, with the sociologist's problem, which points in the opposite direction. Given the data on the frequency of a worker's absence spells and his illness conduct, given these measures for various departments of a firm or over various firms in a country: are we allowed to call departments or firms with a high frequency of illness spells 'sick' or 'ill firms'? do groups of workers who like each other form 'high morale groups', or 'cohesive groups'? Probably both problems, of aggregation and disaggregation depend on some basic assumption of additivity and non-interaction.[27] Yet, the latter term gets a special connotation in sociology as the last examples suggest. There is not only a possibility of statistical interaction but also of interaction as a social process: workers may like each other because they all take a firm stand

27. For econometrists' vision on the aggregation-problems see Edwin Kuhn, 'An essay on aggregation. Theory and practice', in W. Sellekaerts (Ed.) *Econometrics and Economic Theory. Essays in Honour of Jan Tinbergen,* Macmillan, 1974. The problem is, of course, in the focus of attention of econometricians ever since H. Theil's *Linear Aggregation in Economic Relations,* Amsterdam, 1954. Kelvin Lancaster in 'Economic aggregation and additivity' in Krupp's *The Structure of Economic Science* (see our note 6) maintains that there is a two-direction traffic in economics, both going from the macro-theory to micro-variables and trying to discover the implicit restrictions on micro-theory, and the other way round: given micro-theory and micro-variables either posit a macro-theory or try to establish relationships between the macro-variables (p. 203). For a sociological approach see Michael T. Hannan, *Problems of Aggregation and Disaggregation in Sociological Research,* University of North Carolina, 1970; Johan Galtung's *Theory and Methods of Social Research,* Columbia U. Press, 1967, treats the problem under 'the fallacy of wrong level' or 'ecological correlation'. In sociology, the problem was that of disaggregation, at first. While using the census data pertaining to the regions (usually the states, in the United States) as the main source of their evidence, the sociologists between the two wars (1918-1940) applied correlational analysis in order to ascertain the causes of 'fertility of women', of the suicides, of the occurence of mental illness and similar phenomena. Later on, when the emphasis shifted from the analysis of secondary data to the data-gathering in the field (survey and panel studies), aggregation became *the* problem. Another *impetus* came from the social psychological research as represented by group dynamics and from some theoretical streams such as the exchange theory or the interactionism that were basically nominalistic in considering the individual Actor and his decision making as the corner stone of social action.

against the rigid standards imposed by management, thus rejecting group-goals and casting doubts upon the already corroded 'umbrella concept' of group-morale.

Again differences may be of degree rather than of a substantial nature. In the field of research techniques for instance, of sampling and drawing inferences from samples, the two disciplines approach each other. Here again a 'technician', a sampling-statistician, fulfils a useful function of mediator, contributing to the integration of science.

Summing up this already lengthy section, we may state that in the field of analysis of data, interaction and integration prevails over the tendencies towards diversity. At first, each handling their own specific technique (macro-analysis of a system of simultaneous equations in economics, test-construction and multi-variate analysis in psychology, latent-structure analysis or Guttman scaling and application of nonparametric statistics in sociology), the three disciplines exchange their technical know-how, at present. The recognized unity of the linear model (of multiple regression equation system and confirmatory factor analysis), the role which the 'unobserved variables' play in all domains of science and the necessity to deal with the 'measurement error', characterize all three disciplines. So does the attention paid to the treatment of qualitative variables and their inclusion in either multiple regression or hierarchic models. Yet there seems to be a specificity in the approach to measurement problems: the correlation of error terms in economics, estimations of reliability and validity in the test theory, construction of homogeneous (unidimensional) scales in sociology. There also exist different avenues to the problem of aggregation and to the application of mathematics in general (the attempt to introduce dimensional analysis into economics stands comparatively alone).

5.6. Corroboration or immunization of theories

Finally, a few sketchy remarks about the verification process in the sister social sciences. In so far as they are considered positive, empirical disciplines, theories are built in order to deduce hypotheses from them which then are tested empirically. In the opening section we already stated that economics, in contradistinction to the behavioural sciences, is not so unequivocal on this point. Its theories are often ascribed the function of a guideline for practice, are judged to be of a formal, tautological nature. At first glance, economics can be distinguished in this respect from its more empirically minded sisters. Yet, as a young Dutch sociologist argues in a recent article,[28] sociology, too, knows the situation that its protagonists fall in love with their theories and defend these against the facts. Briefly, there are several 'immunization strategies', arguments and procedures how to defend one's own theories *vis à vis* contrary evidence, or how to make them exempt from any evidence, literally 'immune' from anything that can invalidate them. Formal, tautological systems, the truth of which is self evident are one of these strategies. As has been argued, they are more typical of economics than of other social sciences.

Yet even in psychology which acquired experimental criteria of hypotheses testing, 'immunization practices' are not quite strange. For instance, psycho-analytical theory contains hypotheses that are vaguely formulated and virtually untestable, on that account: 'either the presence or the absence of X (e.g. father-identification) leads to Y'. Even where owing to the assumed underlying continuum the X-property exists in various degree and the statement looses its tautological nature, it may remain untestable owing to the difficulty of measuring X precisely enough on at least an ordinal scale to make comparison of the two extreme values with the middle-values meaningful and possible.

In sociology, 'immunization' takes the form either of abstract theories that are devoid of concrete meaning, or the retreat into essentialism, the appeal to the authority of a renowned thinker, etc., etc..[29]

Thus each discipline seems to be characterized by its own 'immunization strategy'. In economics and sociology, the untestable nature of some theoretical premisses is acknowledged and defended as forming part of the basic frame of reference. In psychology, in so far we know, no attempts at their justification are made.

Owing to different levels of quantification, the verification process also differs. In economics, which uses entire systems of prediction equations, it is often possible to verify the assumptions by means of limited observations (better: a few quantitative data). In sociology, where unconnected *ad hoc* hypotheses are tested in one single research design, findings are often inconclusive, sometimes even contradictory. Mo-

28. Wout Ultee, 'The practice of sociology and the abandonment of content as a regulative idea', in *Zeitschrift f. Soziologie*, Jg. 4, 1975, pp. 132-145.
29. *Ibid.*

reover, since the 'rules of correspondence' (that connect operational definitions with the empirical entities) are rather vague, contrary evidence may lead to the redefining of (operational) concepts rather than to the rejection of hypotheses, and the revision of theories. In general, while the creative work of economists is characterized by the preponderance of theoretical thinking over data collection and hypotheses testing, the situation in sociology is just the opposite: fact-finding often lacks theoretical backgrounds, sociologists seldom take pains to formulate alternative theories between which a decision must be taken on grounds of the collected evidence.

5.7. Summary and conclusion

Confronted with the problem of the integration of sociology and economics, we decided to examine the methodologies of the two disciplines in order to assess the communalities and differences of both. Methodology was taken in its broad sense, including decisions about the basic frame-of-reference of a science, the nature of problems it raises, its place in the entire system of sciences, the nature and empirical contents of its theories, its study-designs, and its collection and analysis of data. The results of our comparison are necessarily of a tentative nature. They should be considered as hypotheses about the trends of development of the two sister sciences. These can be tested by content-analysis of the main articles in the representative sociological and economical journals, of the themes of doctoral dissertations, and of books reviewed in the afore-mentioned journals; an enterprise that may be classified under the heading of the sociology of science. The results of our analysis which may be considered as hypotheses in this sense, can be summarized as follows:

1. the principal epistemological problem of economics lies in the delineation of the formal, deductive, logico-normative teaching of rational decision-making concerning the production and distribution of scarce commodities, goods and services, from the empirical study of the same subject. Sociology, on the other hand, is especially concerned with the reconciliation of the dual aspect of its study-subject: the dimension of values, norms and cultural meanings and the external dimension of experiential subjects (persons, vehicals of meanings, material objects, etc., of concrete nature, i.e. situated in the time-space continuum).

2. In sociology description, classification (taxonomy), and interpretation are used much more frequently than in economics. Economics sometimes resorts to instrumentalism, teleology (the chain of ends-and-means relationships) which are, practically unknown in sociology. The categories 'structure' and 'function' are used in formal connotations in economics while they are vested with specific, material meanings in sociology. 'Model' finds but a sporadic use in sociology and denotes there a net of empirical relationships while it is of preponderant importance in economics where it sometimes refers to formal theoretical structure that cannot always directly be confirmed or rejected by the confrontation with empirical facts.

3. Economic analysis chiefly takes place at maeso- or macro-levels while sociologists collect their data from, or through the mediation of, individual persons or families. Problems of data collection receive less attention in economics which deals with secondary data of a quantitative nature. While practically ignoring experimental or quasi-experimental research-designs, economists dispose of powerful statistical techniques to analyse their main variables which are measured at a ratio-level. High demands on the level of measurement lead to the exclusion of possibly relevant variables from their models. This contrasted, until recently, with sociologists who neglected (and still neglect) formal theory formation and dedicated themselves rather to the testing of *ad hoc* hypotheses or of simple models of empirical nature.

4. A trend towards convergence can be noted at present: sociologists embraced path-analysis and dependence analysis that, as econometricians were the first to point out, can efficiently be carried out by applying multiple-regression analysis as available in many computer programs. Some forms of factor analysis are closely related to the linear structural model. Moreover, Theil's logit analysis and Goodman's and Davies' analysis of hierarchical models and of log-linear models converge, too. They extend the field of the construction of causal models to qualitative variables.

Some differences remain: among others, problems of aggregation and disaggregation, different ways of viewing errors in the three sciences.

5. Some minor hypotheses also have been mentioned: those applying mathematical models in their work are less likely to be aware of the philosophical and measurement-assumptions than research workers operating with qualitative variables; more generally, those more frequently applying a certain category of the methodology of science will be

less 'sophisticated', less explicit in the justification of its use.

Thus far a short summary of a few trends formulated here in a hypothetical form. They can be submitted to the content-analysis of the major publications in the two fields, they can also be submitted to criticisms of teams of economists and sociologists. Until they are rejected, the author resorts to his own praxiological device: in order to foster the integration of economics and sociology, both sociologists and economists should learn from each other's methods and techniques of research. Some neglected areas in this field have been stipulated at the end of each section.

6. Anomie and inflation

Tjerk Huppes *

6.1. Introduction

The rate of inflation has risen alarmingly in the last few decades. Intensified efforts to reverse the trend have proved unsuccessful. Even if inflation were stabilized at the level of circa ten percent per annum, prices would double in less than seven years.

Inflation is normally considered to be a subject within the domain of economics. In this paper, however, we have chosen for an interdisciplinary approach. The inflationary process is regarded as an economic manifestation of social disequilibria in a wider sense. Notably, there appears to be a significant relation between the rate of inflation and the degree of anomie in society.

It will be argued that a sociological-economic approach has considerable advantages. Economics, particularly neoclassical macroeconomics, is mainly a theory of equilibrium (section 6.2.). The diverse explanations of inflation, the demand-pull, the cost-push and to a certain extent also the monetary variant, derive from economists who were critical of the equilibrium model (section 6.3.). Inflation is a pre-eminent instance of disequilibrium (section 6.4.). Owing to a historically-grown division of labour in the social sciences, sociology has gained comparative advantages as regards the explanation of disequilibria (section 6.5.).

Anomie is a complex phenomenon. On basis of works by Durkheim and Merton a characterization of anomie in modern sciety is given (section 6.6.). This is followed by a theoretical foundation of the anomie-inflation hypothesis, which in turn will be confronted with figures pertaining to five European countries and the U.S.A. (section 6.7.).

* Thanks is due to Miss D. van der Breggen, who did the preliminary translating work, and to A. Szirmai for his valuable suggestions with respect to the final rendering.

So far economics hasn't succeeded in formulating effective measures against inflation which are at the same time politically feasible. Approaching the problem from the interdisciplinary angle may deepen our understanding of inflation, and may give an impetus to further investigation. Ready-made policy-instruments shouldn't be expected yet (section 6.8.).

6.2. Equilibrium theory in economics

From the very beginning, the economic conceptions of society have been marked by a predominant stress on equilibrium. Adam Smith, already, foresaw a harmonious development of society, brought about by a built-in stabilizer: the 'invisible hand'. Disturbances of equilibrium would be corrected automatically. From Smith to Samuelson, the equilibrium conception has remained the core of economic theory. That economics should have developed in this direction is due to, in particular, Walras, Pareto, and Marshall.

In Walras' equilibrium model, economic life is depicted as a consistent and stationary process of exchange. Consumers maximize utility; manufacturers maximize profits. Nobody has any power; in other words, there is perfect competition.

According to Pareto, an optimal allocation will be attained under these conditions. The market mechanism ensures that the consumers' wishes are translated into a production pattern that satisfies these wishes as effectively as possible. In technical terms: the marginal rates of substitution equal the marginal rates of transformation. In the equilibrium situation no one can improve his position without harming someone else.

Marshall may be regarded as the founding-father of neoclassical economics. His *Principles* (1890) contains a synthesis of 19th century economic thought. The classical theory of supply is combined with the Austrian theory of demand; modern price theory is taking shape. Marshall is rumoured to have said that even a parrot might be turned into an economist, by teaching it merely the words *demand* and *supply*. Up to the 1930s the *Principles* determined the face of economics. Innovators were disqualified with a mere: 'It's all in Marshall'.

After Keynes and World War II the equilibrium theory is reinstated as the 'pièce de résistance' of economics. Emphasis is laid on the theory of growth, as elaborated by Neumann, Meade, Samuelson, Solow and others. Most of the imposing neoclassical models of today in fact still rest on the same traditional foundations: the market mechanism and Say's Law. The concept of equilibrium has been retained, though the terminology has been changed. In the classical view economic behaviour was determined by utilitarianistic motives; the resultant equilibrium was called the 'natural order'. In the neoclassical paradigm economic man maximizes under limiting conditions; in the equilibrium situation prices and incomes reflect the relative scarcity of commodities and factors of production.

Inflation, which is what this paper is about, cannot be explained without amending the harmonious macro-concept. Insight into the problem of inflation may be gained by considering those economists who have, partly or completely, dissociated themselves from the neoclassical conception. Their criticism is directed at the foundation of the general equilibrium model: the market mechanism and Say's Law.

6.3. Inflation

6.3.1. Keynes

'They regard the simplified hypothesis as health, and the further complication as disease'. Thus Keynes in *The end of laissez-faire*. Keynes rejected the neoclassical paradigm. His critical attitude had been prompted by the problem of unemployment in the 1930s.

The orthodox remedies proved ineffective in the face of depression. Cutting down wages should have controlled unemployment by stimulating the demand for labour. This measure would, moreover, lower the prices and increase consumption. To restore equilibrium, the market mechanism had to be propped up a little. The same applied to the capital market, where the rate of interest was apparently too high. If more were saved, the rate of interest would fall, and investments would be reactivated. Colijn testified to his credo: surely the market mechanism could be left to cope.

The fact of the matter was that we sank lower and lower into the depression. Keynes explained why. The classical remedies reduced effective demand. The entrepreneur's revenues thus diminished, which in turn aggravated unemployment. The level of employment is determined by what people buy; not by what can be sold.

With Keynes the situation of full employment never arises automatically, only by coincidence. In principle the national income can stabilize itself at any level, and it's up to the government to fill an eventual gap. The laissez-faire doctrine had to yield to an active budget-policy. Government expenditures and taxes became instrumental variables in the fight to control unemployment.

Keynes' prime concern was to find a solution to the problem of deflation. His model, however, can also be used to explain inflation. In that case, effective demand doesn't fall short, but rather exceeds full employment. Excessive demand pulls up the prices. The well-known remedies for this *demand-pull* inflation are budget-cutting and raising the tax level (functional finance).

Keynes' analysis rests on the assumption that disturbances of equilibrium should be accepted as normal. In contrast to the neoclassical conception, disequilibria require intervention. Yet, in the struggle for control of current inflation, Keynesian economics doesn't offer enough. We shall come to this in section 4.

6.3.2. Marketimperfections and inflation

Marketprices are solely indices of relative scarcity under conditions of perfect competition. This marketform has become rare; yet it is the cornerstone of neoclassical macro-economics. The entrepreneur is assumed to adapt his output to the price-signals of the market. In this case, maximization of profit coincides with the consumers' interest; the marketprices only compensate marginal costs. But if sellers have the power to impose their price on the public, the allocation is no longer optimal. Departures from perfect competition – and there are many – thus cause disharmonies.

The marketform of perfect competition was criticized – once again in the 1930s – by Joan Robinson and Chamberlin. They describe imperfect or monopolistic competition, which corresponds more closely to actual entrepreneur behaviour. Price-setting is the rule, price-taking an exception. The elasticity of demand is variable and allows room for an independent price-policy. Distortions of the allocation emerge; profit-maximization leads to marketprices, which are higher than the marginal costs warrant.

Since Chamberlin and Robinson several other marketforms have been distinguished. The rise of larger firms, for instance, has drawn attention to oligopoly. Popular with social critics, the hobby-horse of neomarxists, this marketform yields considerable opportunities to restrict competition, since the number of competing firms is relatively small.

Formulating laws of oligopolistic market-behaviour is no easy matter. In contradistinction to the other marketforms, the oligopolist has to anticipate on how his competitors are likely to react to his strategy. Their small number causes the action taken by one of them to have direct repercussions on the position of the others. A price-cut will lower the competitor's revenues, and consequently evoke countermeasures. 'The more there is of mine, the less there is of yours'.[1] Chainreactions may vary from a complete price-war to close co-operation. Game-theory offers some support in analyzing oligopolistic behaviour. Empirically verified laws, however, have not emerged so far.

The various forms of imperfect competition have their bearing on the phenomenon of inflation. Perfect competition presupposes that prices come about without being subject to anyone's influence. 'Market-made' prices equal marginal costs. Under conditions of imperfect competition the market mechanism is distorted. The degree of monopoly – price minus marginal costs divided by price – indicates to what extent 'producer-fixed' prices exceed the marginal costs. Thus the pursuit of restricting competition leads to price-increases; power over the market causes inflation (*profit inflation*).

The same argument applies to the labourmarket. An undisturbed working of the market rewards everyone in proportion to his contribution to production. The income distribution corresponds to the marginal productivities of the factors of production. Labour unions, however, restrict competition. Negotiations between employers and unions supersede the market mechanism. If the wage level rises more quickly than overall labour productivity, the risen wage-costs 'push up' the prices (*wage inflation*).[2]

1. To speak with the Duchess in *Alice in Wonderland.*
2. Even a rise of wages equal to the increase in labour productivity may have an inflationary effect. If strongly expanding industries pay as much as their own productivity increase admits, other industries which cannot afford the same wages will have to follow suit and shift the burden to the consumer. In fact the unequal growth of productivity, combined with a more or less central wage policy, may be an important reason for wage inflation.

Once the inflationary process is under way, other complications emerge. The process takes on the semblance of a 'perpetuum mobile', even if all parties involved accept the existing distribution of income. A constant share of labour in the national income requires the wage level to rise with both productivity and prices. The risen wage-costs are in turn followed by new price increases to protect the profit margins. Thus, a rather mechanical pattern of wage- and price increases comes into being: the wage-price spiral.[3] Attempts by labour unions to enlarge the share of labour reinforce the spiral considerably. To improve labour's relative position, wages should rise more quickly than the increase in prices and labour productivity together.

Summarizing our argument so far: marketimperfections cause inflation. Prices go up, because profits have risen, because wage-costs have increased, or, because of a combination of the two. In contradistinction to the Keynesian *demand-pull* inflation, this form of inflation is known as the *cost-push* variant, generated on the supply-side of the market.[4] Sellers (of final products and of production factors) either pass on a diminution of their relative position to others, or try to improve their relative position. The extent to which they control the market determines both their success and the rate of inflation.

In this connection special attention should be paid to the behaviour of oligopolists. In particular, the multinationals are blamed for their contribution to inflation on account of their price-policy. Textbooks tell us that oligopoly is characterized by a kinky demand curve. This would explain why rising costs (for instance through a wage-increase) are passed on to the consumer, whereas productivity-improvements (for instance through technological progress) do not affect the price level.

Avant-guard economists furnish an alternative explanation of the relation between inflation and oligopolistic market strategy. Levinson's view (1972) for example is well-known. According to him, oligopolists – mainly multinationals – aim at maximization of the so-called 'cash-flow' in order to finance further expansion. Increased wage-costs hardly affect the price level on account of the capital-intensive production of the multinationals. Keynesian measures of controlling inflation have an opposite effect; decreasing revenues will entail a rise in prices to sustain

3. Assuming fixed technological coefficients and a constant categorial distribution.
4. In addition, cost-push inflation may result from raised taxes, extension of social securities, the rise of import prices and so on. In these cases, too, the parties concerned try to shift the burden to the consumer.

the cash-flow. In Levinson's view, inflation can be fought successfully, if we remove the obstacles which hinder the realization of the planned cash-flow.

It is mainly the 'off-Broadway' economists who are preoccupied by the role of multinationals in the inflationary process. The mainstream, although aware of marketimperfections, believe that ultimately the market mechanism will have the last word. In the long run prices reflect relative scarcities. The same argument applies to the labour market. Wages exceeding marginal productivity cannot persist. Unemployment arises and thus the disease will burn itself out.

The controversy between neoclassicists and dissidents concerning the true meaning of the market mechanism has flared up again in recent years. This,· however, need not frustrate our understanding of the cost-push inflation. At bottom, it is only of secondary importance whether entrepreneurs are able to control the market for any longer stretch of time. In the same way it is relatively unimportant whether the income distribution, ultimately, corresponds to the relative scarcity of the factors of production. What counts is that labour unions are out to improve labour's relative position, and that entrepreneurs are out to increase profits. These facts in themselves cause inflation. Increased wage-costs result in price increases and vice versa, even if the market, ultimately, determines the allocation.

To convinced 'market-economists' it is self-evident that the wage-price spiral is caused by shortsightedness concerning the workings of the market. In this view the aspirations of both entrepreneurs and unions are irrational. The conflict between both parties will eventually be decided by the market. The spiral is a sad side-effect of a fight against windmills.

It was Pareto, who applied the distinction between rational and irrational behaviour as a criterion for the division of labour between economics and sociology. Economics should study the rational component of human behaviour: his optimum theorem assumes rational behaviour. The remainder, irrational behaviour, was assigned to the domain of sociology. To Pareto, disturbances in the market should be put down to sociological variables. The distinction between rational and irrational behaviour as a criterion for the division of labour between economics and sociology has become outdated. What remains is the potential contribution of sociology to our understanding of marketimperfections and their corollary: inflation.

6.3.3. Monetary inflation

Monetary disturbances of equilibrium have been described long before the rise of economics as a science. Dating back to the 16th century is the well-known *naive* quantity theory of Bodin and Davanzati. The relationship they found between the price level and the supply of money was refined by Irving Fisher in 1911. His MV = PT may be found in any handbook. Several causes of monetary disturbances are contained in this single formula: changes in the quantity of money by borrowing and lending, and in the velocity of money by hoarding and dishoarding. Contributions to the development of monetary theory have been made, in particular, by Wicksell, Marshall, Robertson, Keynes and Von Hayek. At present Milton Friedman is its most distinguished representative.

Most monetarists are closely allied to the neoclassical paradigm.[5] In its most rudimentary form monetary theory comes down to the following. Prices by and large reflect relative scarcity, the rate of interest excluded. The bankers are the chief obstructionists. They manipulate the rate of interest below its 'natural' level, thus inducing investors and consumers to spend more money. This leads to an excessive creation of money (*monetary inflation*). Well known tools to control monetary inflation are: open market sales of securities, raising the minimum reserve requirements of commercial banks, raising the central bank's rate of interest, etc..

The question remains whether monetary policy is capable of curbing current inflation. In most western countries the monetary authorities pursue a responsible monetary policy. Nevertheless the rate of inflation has been going up. The number of experts inclined to be sceptical gradually outweighs those who take a more optimistic view; the more so, now that the monetary policy in the U.S.A. has proved a failure. Increased liquidities are considered to be far more the result of inflation, rather than an autonomous cause. The quantity of money is more of less compelled to give way.

5. 'The following metaphor may clarify things: with regard to Say's Law, monetary theorists (like Hayek and Hawtrey) can be considered heretics. They believe in it, but their belief is marred by certain aberrations. Keynesians can't be accused of heresy; they just don't believe'. J. Pen, *Moderne Economie,* 1968, p. 152.

6.4. Current inflation

The price level of private consumption in the Netherlands rose

from 1955 to 1960 by 2,6% p.a.,
from 1960 to 1965 by 3,6% p.a.,
from 1965 to 1970 by 4,4% p.a.,
from 1970 to 1975 by 8,5% p.a..

In spite of concentrated efforts the government has not succeeded in reversing this trend. It seems that economics cannot offer an adequate solution for the present inflation. The lessons from the past are not worth much either. Spectacular price increases, caused by the issue of the 'assignations' at the time of the French Revolution, by the 'green backs' during the American Civil War, or after World War I in Germany and Russia, have little in common with contemporary inflation. These disruptions were caused by the authorities, creating money to an irresponsible degree. The hyperflation of the early days was usually a form of monetary pathology.

The post-war inflationary process is of a specific nature. After the creeping inflation in the 1950s its pace has quickened alarmingly. In contrast to former times, governments and monetary authorities nowadays know what they have to do. Nevertheless the tools have failed. Neither Keynesian nor monetary policies can hold back the flood. At the same time, moreover, increasing unemployement considerably restricts the ways in which inflation might be fought. The double-edged sword of rising prices and unemployment – also known by the term stagflation – characterizes modern inflation. The confidence in the 'old-time religion of budget-cutting and tight money'[6] is dwindling, while at the same time there are no acceptable alternatives available.

Zijlstra puts the problem as follows: 'The fact that there is no reason why the inflationary process should reverse in the future is what's most alarming about the whole situation. The crux of the matter is that the power of certain groups to push up wages and prices has become greater than that of governments and central banks to restrain them'.[7]

6. *Time Magazine*, October 1974, p. 40.
7. J. Zijlstra, *Rede voor de jaarvergadering van de Bank voor Internationale Betalingen*, 1970.

Zijlstra is one of the many economists who consider cost-push inflation as the chief malefactor. We have shown this variant to be the result of marketimperfections. Marketcontrol, in particular of employers and labour unions, causes wages and prices to rise. The state is not able to break their power. The resulting wage-price spiral becomes an autonomous process.

Yet an effective weapon against inflation is conceivable. In most western countries the government has power to promulgate wage- and price-controls. In theory inflation could be pulled up short tomorrow. But who dares pull the emergency-brake? The mere threat of pulling it causes trouble, as former Dutch administrations have experienced to their detriment. Illustrative of the attitude of many politicians is a statement by President Ford at his first press conference: 'Wage and price controls are out, period!'

In short, there is no reason to be optimistic. Economic solutions have proved either ineffective or politically unfeasible. The recent mammoth-debate in the United States in September 1974 has made this clear once again. The proposed remedies were restricted to variations on the demand-pull, cost-push and monetary theory. Hopeful alternative suggestions were not heard.

Top American economists yielded to the same gloomy view: 'that the battle against roaring inflation will be long and painful, and during its course the nation will suffer a protracted period of stagnant production and rising unemployment that by any name will amount to a recession'.[8]

The following diagnosis now stands to reason. Apparently the inflationary process is affected by variables which are outside the world of economic abstraction. The problem to be solved has been inadequately conceptualized. This view fits in with the state of affairs in economics as described above. The analytical apparatus is first and foremost attuned to the analysis of equilibrium. Comparatively little attention is paid to the phenomenon of disequilibrium, with which our rapidly changing society is so richly endowed. In order to explain the causes of disequilibrium one must look – like Pareto did – beyond economics. Reading Hartog we find: '... that inflation is not a purely economic problem ... Much more might be said for the view that inflation is the economic manifestation of disturbances of equilibrium, which have their roots in a social and political substratum ... Likewise, controlling

8. *Time Magazine*, October 1974, p. 40.

inflation with purely economic means won't do, as the underlying causes are not affected'.[9] We tend to agree with Hartog. The inflationary process is the economic manifestation of a disequilibrium, the meaning of which can't be fully grasped without consulting the social sciences. The central hypothesis of this paper is based on this interdisciplinary insight. Anticipating what follows we shall assume a positive significant relation between the rate of inflation on the one hand, and the degree of anomie on the other. This hypothesis will be confronted with the computed correlations between a number of operationally defined indicators of anomie and the increase in the price level of private consumption, as measured in the last two decades in five European countries and the United States.

The argument will be built up as follows. After pointing to the 'comparative advantages' of sociology in relation to the explanation of social disturbances, an analysis of anomie will be given. After that the anomie-inflation hypothesis will be theoretically grounded and empirically verified.

6.5. Sociology versus economics

The rise of economics coincided with the Industrial Revolution of the latter half of the 18th century. More than fifty years elapsed after Adam Smith's *Wealth of Nations,* before Auguste Comte laid the foundations of sociology in his *Cours de Philosophie Positive.* Both academic disciplines studied society with a view to formulating general laws. Their methods were modelled on those of the physical sciences. At first Comte even spoke of 'social physics'.

However, the way in which each of them interpreted social phenomena differed fundamentally. Adam Smith was a convinced adherent of the principle of 'laissez-faire'. As a result of the workings of an 'invisible hand' a 'natural order' would develop in society. 'What ought to be' and 'what is' automatically converge.[10] After Smith, a more dramatic impact of the Industrial Revolution on social life became manifest. The belief in a harmonious development of society receded; a precondition for the rise of sociology.

9. F. Hartog, *Inflatie: oorzaken, gevolgen, bestrijding.* Alphen aan de Rijn 1966, p. 58-59.
10. The distinction 'ought-is' is related to 'the political element in the development of economic theory' by G. Myrdal. See his book of the same title, London 1953, p. 5ff.

In Comte's work the acknowledgement that norms and values are relative is a recurrent theme. In his view there is no such thing as a 'natural state or order'. Society evolves; every order is relative to time and place. For Comte, the search for laws of society should be connected with their application in the service of social progress. 'Savoir pour prévoir, et prévoir pour pouvoir'. A harmonious evolution doesn't arise by itself; it is the result of effective control. To this end insight should be gained into social processes. It's for sociology to reveal the regularities to which society obeys.

The difference between sociology and economics became more prominent as each discipline developed its own independent system of thought. Economic theory dissociated itself from sociological variables, and stuck to a concept of society in which equilibrium plays a predominant part. Sociology was concerned with social disturbances caused by technological development and the advancing division of labour. Marx was the last to design a sociological-economic theory of society. In economics he has mainly inspired dissidents. His influence on distinguished sociologists, however, is undeniable.

Round the turn of the century the separation of the two disciplines had become complete. In these years, Walras, Marshall and Pareto (as economist) gave shape to the neoclassical paradigm. The explanation of economic phenomena by means of the equilibrium-concept is given a formal and a-historical character. The institutional structure is considered a datum. The influence of social disturbances on economic processes is regarded as irrelevant. In fact, neoclassical economics, following Smith, has equated the existing order with the 'natural order'.

Also around 1900, Durkheim, Max Weber and Pareto (as sociologist) saw another reality. It was the imbalances of industrialized societies, that intrigued them. To Durkheim the defective functioning of organic solidarity led to anomie; Weber emphasized de-personalization resulting from rationalization and bureaucratization; while, in his later work, Pareto attached great importance to the struggle for power caused by the irrational component of human behaviour. These sociologists have more in common with one another than their diverging terminology allows for. Society is having difficulties in adjusting to the progress of science and technology. The ensuing problems are formulated in different ways. Mannheim and Sorokin, tackling the same kind of problems, form the link between Weber and modern sociology.

Surveying the developments in the field of economics and sociology, a systematic difference in approach becomes apparent. Compared with economics, sociology pays more attention to imbalances in industrial societies. This preoccupation of sociologists is important with respect to the explanation of the inflationary process; an outstanding example of disequilibrium. Economics has failed to come up with an adequate answer. On account of the historically-grown division of labour between the two disciplines, sociology seems well-equipped to broaden and deepen our understanding of the problem of inflation.

6.6. Anomie

6.6.1. Durkheim

The concept of anomie was introduced into sociology by Emile Durkheim. He used it to indicate a crisis situation of a society, an institution or a group. To elucidate the meaning of the term a brief summary of his work will be given.

Durkheim's programme of study, the overriding problem in all his work, concerns the sources of social order and disorder, the forces that make for regulation or de-regulation in the body social. Whereof – Durkheim asked himself – does the specific cohesion consist, which is implied in the word 'society'.

In answering this question, he made a most relevant distinction between two kinds of society: the pre-industrial, comparatively stable society and the industrialized, dynamic society. The social cement in the more simple social structure is indicated by the term 'mechanical solidarity'. It is based on a homogeneous system of norms and values, together forming the so-called 'conscience collective', which last concept is comparable to Rousseau's 'volonté générale', Comte's 'consensus' and, to some extent, even to Adam Smith's 'natural order'. In primitive types of society a common 'conscience collective' keeps everyone's aspirations in check. Traditional rules and restrictions constitute a regulative force; vertical mobility is practically non-existent. Countenanced by moral authorities (like, for instance, the church) poor and rich alike accept the historically-grown social order. The individual doesn't distinguish between society as it is, and as it should be. The 'conscience collective' and the 'conscience individuelle' are one and the same.

With the Industrial Revolution a new era begins. The progress of science and technology brings about radical changes. The authority of traditional moral institutions crumbles. The social order is no longer automatically taken for granted; neither are rigid social controls. More than before it is possible for the individual to develop his faculties as he thinks fit. Individual thought emancipated itself from the 'conscience collective'. Because of the division of labour a different kind of social cohesion comes into existence, the so-called 'organic solidarity'. It results from the complementarity of the specialized functions of the production process. In themselves specialized activities have no meaning; the participants must produce together. This interdependence enhances internal cohesion. Industrial society is characterized by structural integration.

At first Durkheim thought that organic solidarity was sufficient guarantee for an integrated social life. In his later work he is much more pessimistic. The division of labour isn't capable of controlling human relationships adequately. The weakening of the 'conscience collective' gives rise to a condition of relative normlessness: anomie. This phenomenon is measurable in several ways. In Durkheim's work the rate of suicide in societies serves as an index of the degree of integration.

Durkheim distinguished several kinds of suicide. Firstly there is the so-called egoistic suicide, the result of the weaknesses of organic solidarity. The second kind is the anomic suicide,[11] caused by insufficient mechanic solidarity. More important than the distinction between these types is the common hypothesis underlying both of them: 'the rate of suicide varies inversely to the degree of integration of social groups of which the individual is part'.[12] This hypothesis is based on the outcome of Durkheim's researches. The suicide-percentage among non-Catholics is higher than among Catholics; among the unmarried higher than among the married, etc.. Since the first publication of 'Le Suicide' in English, in 1951, scientific research has received a new stimulus to investigate the phenomenon of suicide.[13] By and large the results have borne out

11. A third type – altruistic suicide – is less relevant to our purposes. Well-known examples are: The Samuri, who committed suicide for their lord; the Kamikase pilots, who dashed themselves to pieces on military goals; the Hindu widows, who followed their deceased husbands in death. A fourth type – fatalistic suicide – is touched upon only briefly in Durkheim's work.

12. E. Durkheim, *Le Suicide,* 1897, p. 223.

13. Cf. L.I. Dublin, *Suicide: A Sociological and Statistical Study,* New York, 1963. J.P. Gibbs and W.T. Martin, *Status integration and Suicide,* Oregon 1964.

Durkheim's hypothesis. A significant rise in the rate of suicide correlates with a weakening of the social cohesion.

Important for the concept of anomie is finally Durkheim's sociology of religion,[14] a subject to which he devoted the last few years of his life. Durkheim acknowledged the pre-eminently integrating function of religious norms and values. 'Religion is an eminently collective thing'.[15] The increasing irreligiousness implied that the 'conscience collective' was being impaired. Like Ivan Karamazov, the agnostic Durkheim asked himself: 'Once God is dead, does not everything become permissible?' His sagacious answer may be paraphrased as follows.

Man is a social being. Social existence is impossible without entering into relationships with one's fellowmen. In every society there are norms regulating these relationships. Norms restrict the possible modes of behaviour. An adult accepts these restrictions; he has internalized the norms. In fact, his 'conscience individuelle' is a reflection of the 'conscience collective' of society. 'Society is something beyond us and something in ourselves'.[16] It is due to society that we are what we are. Thus man is existentially dependent on the society in which he happens to live.[17] Through religion, the power of society over the individual is projected into a transcendental supreme being. In God, man experiences his dependence on society. Obedience to the 'conscience collective' is translated into obedience to a power over and above society.[18] God is society, or rather, its symbolic representation.

A. Pierce, The Economic Cycles and the Sociological Suicide Rate, *The American Sociological Review,* 1967.

14. E. Durkheim, *The Elementary Forms of Religious Life,* New York, 1954.

15. *Ibid.,* p. 47.

16. E. Durkheim, *Sociology and Philosophy,* New York, 1953, p. 55.

17. Freud's 'Superego' is comparable to Durkheim's 'conscience individuelle'. The 'Superego' is our conscience, the seat of authority which informs the 'Ego' about socially acceptable possibilities to satisfy the desires of the 'Id'. The 'Superego' develops during the upbringing. The child, so to speak, internalizes the 'conscience collective'. The Freudian child-parent relationship, in which the child is dependent on the parents, resembles Durkheim's relationship between individual and society.

18. In his early work Marx calls the projection of the power of society into a supreme being, beyond the control of man, alienation. 'Objectification is the practice of alienation ... man, so long as he is engrossed in religion, can only objectify his essence – Homo Faber – by an alien and fantastic being'. (Karl Marx, *Early Writings,* trans. and ed. by T.B. Bottomore, New York 1964). Disregarding his revolutionary goals, Marx's view is not incompatible with Durkheim's. Religion is conducive to social integration; both authors are agreed on that. Marx, however, takes a negative view of this, because he wants to break the (to his mind unjust) status-quo. The conservative power of religion serves to disguise the abuse of power by the capitalists. Thus religion becomes opium for the people.

Is it true now that increasing irreligiousness must needs be attended by anomie? Durkheim answers in the negative. 'We must discover the rational substitutes for these religious notions that for a long time have served as the vehicle for the most essential moral ideas'.[19] Secularization will only result in disintegration, if no substitute is found. In terms of modern sociology, Durkheim points to the possibility of functional alternatives for a religious code.

Besides religion, other behaviour-controlling codes are conceivable. Ideologies, for instance, may preserve social cohesion as well. The 20th century has provided more than one example; the most extreme being Nazi-Germany and Mao's China.[20]

Durkheim, however, was by no means an advocate of a collectivistic solution to anomic tendencies. Notwithstanding the signs of disintegration, which he observed in his time, he preferred the freedom of the individual to conformism.[21] Nor did he pine for the pre-industrial society with its protective, but impulse-stifling rigidities. In his political sociology Durkheim attempts a compromise, rejecting both excessive individualization and rigid social control as incompatible with self-realization.

6.6.2. Merton

Since Durkheim, anomie has become one of the key concepts of sociology. After World War II (by-passing the crisis literature of the

19. E. Durkheim, *Moral Education*, New York, 1961, p. 9.
20. An excerpt from a broadcast by radio Peking on December 6th, 1967 might serve as an illustration: 'Every river flows into the sea and every red heart turns to the sun. Oh, Chairman Mao, Chairman Mao, mountains are high, but not so high as the blue sky. Rivers are deep, but not so deep as the ocean. Lights are bright, but not so bright as the sun. Your goodness is loftier than the sky, deeper than the ocean and brighter than the sun. One can count the stars in the furthermost skies, but it's impossible to count your contributions to mankind'. Maoism as 'the message'; Mao as 'the enlightened saviour'. If one prefers: the 'droit divin' in a 20th century neomarxian rendering. Charismatic leadership and leaderworship are, from the functional point of view, alternatives to a religious code. Both ideologies and religious convictions are capable of safeguarding the integration of society.
21. This appears most clearly from his article in responce to the Dreyfus-case. According to Neyer:
'It presents the doctrine of the sacredness of the individual in a concentrated form, and spares us the task of bringing together all the references to it that are scattered throughout Durkheim's works'. J. Neyer, Individualism in Durkheim, in: K.H. Wolf, ed., *Emile Durkheim 1858-1917*, Columbus, 1960.

interwar period) a spate of publications on anomie appears, especially in the United States.[22] In most of them, anomie is regarded as an integral part of modern society. Merton's much-quoted *Social Structure and Anomie* is no doubt the most influential.[23] Like Parsons, the founder of functionalism in sociology, Merton regards the 'goals and normative standards which people acquire while living in society' as the most important aspects of social action. Anomie is the result of a dissociation between the 'culturally prescribed aspirations (goals) and the socially structured avenues (norms) for realizing these aspirations'.[24] The 'money success goal' is overaccentuated in the United States. 'A cardinal American virtue, ambition, promotes a cardinal American vice, deviant behaviour'.[25] 'Internalized norms' acquire the meaning of 'external constraints'. The individual disregards the obtaining norms, which hinder him in attaining his objectives. The end justifies the means; those who conform might fail. Under conditions like these 'institutional norms' lose their control over behaviour (disinstitutionalization). Thus anomie arises, specified by Merton into different forms of deviant behaviour: innovation, ritualism, retreatism and rebellion.

Three points of difference between Merton and Durkheim deserve attention. Merton's anomie is closely related to the more general concept of deviant behaviour. While Durkheim especially used the rate of suicide as an indicator of social disintegration, Merton emphasized phenomena like crime, delinquency, mental illness, bohemianism, etc. This distinction is relevant to the verification of our anomie-inflation hypothesis. In making a selection of anomie-indicators, both authors have been taken into account.

Secondly, in contrast to Durkheim, Merton lards his argument with references to the psychological aspects of anomie. Freud, Horney, Sullivan, McIver, Riesman, and others are mentioned. The psychological dimension of anomie may be characterized as follows.

The 'Superego' or 'conscience individuelle' of every social actor contains a number of internalized norms, regulating the satisfaction of the 'Id' impulses. The normative standards restrict behaviour alternatives, thus enabling the individual to engage in meaningful relationships. Groups consist of individuals with similar standards; identification with

22. Vide the bibliography in: H.P.M. Goddijn, *Anomie,* Leiden, 1970, pp. 66-76.
23. R.K. Merton, *Social Theory and Social Structure,* New York, 1956, pp. 131-195.
24. *Ibid.*, p. 134.
25. *Ibid.*, p. 146.

the group makes it easier for the members to maintain normative standards.

Modern society consists of a great variety of groups, each with their own normative code. This is expressed in terms like normative complexity, heterogeneity, poly-valence, differentiation and so on. The normative content of these groups, moreover, is subject to rapid change. The combination of normative complexity and rapid social change,[26] disrupts the individual's commitment to a set of norms, and thereby his sense of identity. Internalized norms are no longer something to go by.[27] Conflicts between both the groups to which the individual belongs[28] and between members of the same group, throw him back upon himself. It is true that the freedom of self-determination has increased. This very freedom, however, reactivates feelings of solitude, meaninglessness, anxiety and aggression as the possibilities of identification become less and less.[29] 'Anomie is a state of mind in which the individual's sense of social cohesion – the mainspring of his morale – is broken or fatally weakened'.[30] Under conditions like these, crime, delinquency, mental illness, bohemianism, etc., will increase.

A third difference between Durkheim and Merton. Merton hardly touches upon the origins of anomie. Both the discrepancy between 'money success goal and institutional norms', and the ensuing forms of deviant behaviour are regarded as specifications of the anomic character

26. '... (Under) conditions of great normative complexity and/or rapid social change individuals are pulled this way and that by numerous conflicting norms and goals, until the person is literally disorientated and de-moralized, unable to secure a firm commitment to a set of norms that he can feel as self-consistent'.
R.M. Williams Jr., *American Society,* New York, 1951, p. 535.
Quoted by R.K. Merton, *Social theory and Social Structure,* New York, 1965, p. 190.

27. 'It appears unlikely that cultural norms, once interiorized, are wholly eliminated. Whatever residuum persists will induce personality tensions and conflict, with some measure of ambivalence. A manifest rejection of the once-incorporated institutional norms will be coupled with some latent retention of their emotional correlates. Guilt feeling, a sense of sin, pangs of conscience are diverse terms referring to this unrelieved tension. Symbolic adherence to the nominally repudiated values or rationalizations for the rejection of these values constitute a more subtle expression of the tensions'. R.K. Merton, *Social Theory and Social Structure,* New York, 1957 p. 136.

28. 'If the groups of an individual are in conflict; if they urge him to contradictory actions, duties, thoughts, convictions; ... the respective egos will be mutual antagonistic. The individual will be a house divided against himself, split by inner conflicts ... He will be like a ball pushed in opposite directions by several forces'. P.A. Sorokin, *Society, Culture and Personality,* New York, 1947, p. 351.

29. Cf. E. Fromm, *Escape from Freedom,* New York, 1941.

30. R.M. McIver, *The Ramparts We Guard,* New York, 1950, p. 84.

of American society. The development from integration to disintegration remains unexplained. In this respect Durkheim's explanation is more satisfactory. According to him, the advancing division of labour is the main causal factor. The social changes it brings about – such as for instance the growing differentiation – results in a situation of relative normlessness.

With respect to our hypothesis the causes of anomie are of secondary importance. We only assume a positive significant relation between the rate of inflation and the degree of anomie. Explaining the causes of anomie is, strictly speaking, outside the scope of our present issue. In order to be complete, however, we will give it some attention.

Science and technology have often been regarded by sociologists as the motor of social development. Innovations bring about social changes; the retarded adjustment of norms, values and institutions – the cultural lag – gives rise to conflicts. In economics it is especially institutionalists such as Galbraith, Heilbroner, Myrdal, Gruchy and others who, following Veblen,[31] attach great value to the causal chain: 'advancing technology – retarding institutional change – conflict'. As applied to the post-war period, Heilbroner[32] speaks of 'the revolutionary power of science and scientifically based technology', which will eventually sap the institutional structures of western society.

Heilbroner is no optimist; in his most recent work[33] he even predicts that mankind will come to the same end as Goethe's apprentice. Apart from that, his analysis does give insight into the process of change which is taking place in the western world. The explosive development of science and technology, especially in the last few decades, confronts society with serious problems of adaptation.[34] The number of conflicts is on the increase.

This brings us to another aspect of anomie. Anomie involves conflicts.

31. 'The science and technology available to society, determine the character of its culture ... Institutions are products of the past process, are adapted to past circumstances, and are therefore never in full accord with the requirements of the present. Those who have a vested interest in the old order will bend every effort to maintain old institutions even when they are no longer in tune with technological requirements'.
T. Veblen, *The theory of the Leisure class,* 1934, p. 191.

32. R.L. Heilbroner, *The limits of American Capitalism,* 1966, p. 154.

33. R.L. Heilbroner, *An inquiry into the human prospect,* 1974.

34. An obvious example is the technical progress in the field of medical science; norm-uncertainty has risen, in particular among religious denominations, concerning abortion, birth control, euthanasia etc.

In a stable community consensus prevails. Generally accepted norms support the institutional structure and sanction the exercise of power. Modern society is in a constant process of change. Renewal of the institutions that are becoming obsolete, is necessary. During this process the power hierarchy is in a state of disorder. Vested interests retard the adjustment of the institutional structure. The exercise of power is experienced as coercion, thus involving conflict.

Groups living in conflict with each other or with society as a whole, internally often exhibit a strong sense of cohesion and strict social control. Anomie on macro-level has its antipode in conformistic behaviour on micro-level. When the obtaining norms lose their regulating function, groups with a firm cohesive structure afford fresh opportunities of identification. Such groups may contribute to necessary reforms and adjustments. But often they also have escape functions for their members, offering action as a protection against anomic confusion.

6.6.3. Anomie and modern society

Anomie is a complex phenomenon. Its essential characteristics can be summarized on the basis of a number of interrelated dichotomies, which will moreover enable us to give a characterization of modern western society.

Stationary versus dynamic. As changes in normative standards occur more rapidly anomie will become more widespread in society. Obtaining norms lose their regulating function, without new norms having sufficiently developed to give much support. The acceleration so characteristic of western society these last few decades may perhaps be imputed to the explosive development in the fields of science and technology.[35] Research on possible causal relations, however, is outside the scope of this paper.

35. The advance of science and technology may also play a part in determining the direction in which society is developing. Via secularization (demystification) science and technology lead to democratization and equalization. The justification of differences in power by religion (for instance: 'le droit divin') is diminishing. Ritual marks of authority are on the wane (ministers and professors become plain 'mister'; the G.P. takes off his white coat; the monk disrobes). This process of equalization also has its bearing on the part of the social hierarchy expressed in money: the distribution of income. In those countries, for instance, where social life is strongly influenced by the church (Spain, Portugal, Greece, South-America) the distribution of income appears to be more unequal than is the case in

Homogeneous versus heterogeneous, differentiated, pluralistic or complex. As the norms of individuals and groups diverge more and more, the cohesion of society is impaired. In Durkheim's terms: mechanical solidarity is replaced by organic solidarity, while the latter is an insufficient guarantee for an integrated social life. Durkheim sees the advancing division of labour as the main cause of this lack of integration. Generally speaking, advances in science and technology seem to parallel the degree of normative complexity.

Conformism (social control) versus deviant behaviour (individualization). In a rapidly changing, complex society social control on macro-level diminishes, whereas deviant behaviour is on the increase. In a situation of relative normlessness it is not immediately clear, though, which kind of behaviour should be designated as deviant. The number of homicides, suicides, property crimes, etc., however, remain undisputable indicators of relative normlessness. In the following section we shall see that these phenomena of late have become more frequent.

Solidarity versus psychic conflicts. On the plane of the individual, growing norm-instability deepens feelings of loneliness, meaninglessness, anxiety and aggression. Norms regulate the emotional drives; changes in normative standards disrupt the commitment to social relationships and necessitate reorientation. The highly increased number of divorces, for instance, illustrates this process. Reorientation involves psychic tensions and conflicts. The increase in the consumption of psychopharmaca would be a good indicator of the mounting stress under which people live.[36] The anomie-indicators mentioned above, for that matter, may also be regarded as manifestations of disturbed relationships.

Legitimate power (authority, consensus) versus non-legitimated power (coercion, conflict). Power is unevenly distributed in any society. When sanctioned by internalized norms, power manifests itself as authority. A change in normative standards makes adjustment of the institutional structure necessary, which process is retarded by vested interests. During the period of change the exercise of power is experienced as coercion. The so-called 'crisis of authority', and its corollary conflict, may be noted in various sectors of contemporary western society. A precise measuring of the frequency of conflicts would necessitate

more secularized countries (Norway, Sweden, Denmark, Holland, North-America). The relation 'science and technology – equalization' would repay further investigation.

36. Unfortunately, there are no precise data available on the consumption of psychopharmaca.

extensive research. For this reason the frequency of conflict is less suitable for us as an indicator, as the inquiry into the correlation between anomie and inflation has been restricted to available secondary sources.

6.7. Anomie and inflation

6.7.1. Theoretical foundations

Human action is directed towards satisfaction of wants. These wants exceed the means of satisfying them. People have to make choices.

Economists usually analyse human action from this perspective. Economic action means choosing from scarce means which have alternative uses. Market prices confront the economic subject with the fact that the means of satisfaction are limited. In the neoclassical equilibrium model it is assumed that these restrictions are taken for granted. Prices (and incomes) come about through the workings of the market mechanism on which the individual has no demonstrable influence.

Human action, from the sociological angle, is definable in much the same way. Not prices, but normative standards restrict the alternative modes of behaviour. Early in life – during socialization – man is confronted with these restrictions. The unbrideled impulses of a child meet with countless obstacles, which, as the socialization process advances, assume a more or less self-evident character. Norms that have thus been internalized, will guide the grown up in his conscious and unconscious choices. Normative standards are maintained because of a process of social control on which the individual has no demonstrable influence.

Norms and prices may thus be regarded in the same light. Both impose restrictions on the alternative modes of behaviour in the quest for the satisfaction of wants; both regulate human intercourse. In a postulated condition of equilibrium, prices reflect the consumers' preferences owing to the workings of the marketmechanism, whereas norms correspond to the desired social behaviour owing to the process of social control.[37] The

37. Hans Albert, among others, has drawn attention to the correspondence between the marketmechanism and the process of social control: 'Es dürfte kaum übertrieben sein zu

economic subject is pricetaker, the social actor conforms: restrictions are taken for granted, economically as well as sociologically. In this light, what is the relationship between anomie and inflation?

What is inflation? In the preceding three variants have been reviewed: demand-pull, cost-push and monetary inflation.

Demand-pull inflation arises when effective demand exceeds full employment (full capacity). Consumers, investors and the government together want more than is feasible (disregarding foreign trade). Cost-push inflation is caused by the conflict about the distribution of income. Everybody wants more; no one wants to stay behind. With this variant it is the factors of production who together want more than is feasible. Monetary inflation arises when the monetary authorities are unable or unwilling to restrict the money supply. The present increase in the stock of money, however, should be regarded as a result rather than an autonomous cause of inflation.

It goes without saying that the various types of inflation always concern the same people, acting as consumers, income-earners, members of pressure groups, etc.. Without blaming any one group in particular, inflation may be said to be caused by the fact that all of us together want more than is feasible. The regulating function of the market mechanism is diminishing. The restrictions of the status quo are being increasingly disregarded.

What is anomie? A complex phenomenon the essence of which is best expressed by the term relative normlessness. It develops in a rapidly changing complex society. The prevailing norms lose their controlling function, while in the restriction of alternative modes of behaviour, the new normative standards offer too little to go by. Once internalized norms, come to be experienced as external constraints. Social control crumbles. The restrictions of the status quo are being increasingly disregarded.

Thus the economic phenomenon of inflation and the sociological phenomenon of anomie may be regarded as aspects of the same process of social change.

behaupten, dass in Adam Smith Konzeption der 'unsichtbare Hand' eigentlich eine kybernetische Idee der sozialen Kontrolle steckt, die ihre Bedeutung auch dann behält, wenn man sie aus ihrem teilweise metaphysische-ideologischen Hintergrund herauslöst und von der mehr oder weniger normativen Spekulation über die Optimalität der dadurch zustandgekommen Ordnung des sozialen Geschehens abstrahiert, einer Spekulation, der letzte Ausläufer in der Wohlfahrtsökonomie zu finden sind'.
Hans Albert, *Marktsoziologie und Entscheidungslogik*, 1967, p. 395.

The theoretical connection between anomie and inflation may be extended in various directions.

	stability	anomie - inflation
norms	generally accepted norms regulate social behaviour; the status quo is accepted	norms lose their regulating function; the status quo restrictions are being increasingly disregarded
prices	generally accepted 'market'-prices regulate economic behaviour; the status quo is accepted	'market'-prices lose their regulating function; the status quo restrictions are being increasingly disregarded
social control	the process of social control maintains stability	social control diminishes; various types of deviant behaviour increase; so does the number of conflicts
market mechanism	the market mechanism maintains stability	the allocation by the market mechanism decreases (in both the market of final products and productive factors); the number of 'deviant' prices increases (prices exceed marginal costs); so does the number of conflicts
distribution of power	the institutionalized power structure is legitimated by internalized norms	the institutionalized power structure is challenged; it is no longer legitimated by internalized normative standards; the exercise of power is experienced as coercion; vested interests retard adjustment
distribution of income	the distribution of income resulting from the working of the market-mechanism is accepted as such	the distribution of income is challenged; the 'market'-distribution is no longer experienced as self-evident but as unjust; equalization is resisted by passing on the risen wage-costs

Deviant behaviour and cost-push inflation. If we accept the conceptual correspondance between the market mechanism and social control (respectively between prices and norms) another relation emerges: that between deviant behaviour and cost-push inflation.

Prices that have been established in the market reflect the marginal costs (including a 'normal' profit). Marketimperfections lead to price-increases (section 6.3.2); both entrepreneurs and unions refuse to conform to the laws of the market. By fixing deviating prices they either try to improve their relative positions, or to shift an impending diminution of their positions to others.

This process of restricting the market mechanism runs parallel to a weakening of social control. As the non-conformist breaks from generally observed normative standards, so the price-setter endeavours to ignore the laws of the market. Deviant social behaviour (anomie) and deviant market behaviour (inflation) are similar phenomena, if studied by distinct academic disciplines.

Conflicts of power and cost-push inflation. Apart from the conceptual correspondence between prices and norms, the market mechanism and social control, there is finally the possibility of drawing a similar parallel between the distribution of income and the power hierarchy.[38] In the process of social change and its corollary anomie, it is not only the power hierarchy that will be questioned, but also the existing income distribution. The distribution of income may be regarded as the part of the power hierarchy expressed in money. The retarding of institutional innovations by vested interests is the sociological counterpart of the resistance to income-levelling in the guise of passed-on risen wage-costs. Social conflicts and cost-push inflation thus run paralle.

6.7.2. Research findings*

Inflation is attended with anomie and vice versa. In concreto, a positive significant relation is assumed between the annual inflation percentages and the annually measured values of a number of anomie-indicators. Firstly, this relation will be confronted with figures pertaining to the Netherlands and the United States. The collected data for the Netherlands refer to the period of 1955-1974 (table 1); those for the United States to 1960-1974 (table 2, the anomie-figures prior to 1960 are differently classified from those coming after; the two sets can't be reduced to one another).

The investigation has been restricted to data from secondary sources. The C.B.S. statistics as well as the U.S. Statistical Abstracts supply

38. The relation between prices – norms, marketmechanism – social control, distribution of income – allocation of power has been treated at length in chapter two of this book.

* I am indebted to Jankees de Graaf for having performed the computations in this section.

Table 1a. Inflation (incl. smoothed average) and anomie-indicators the Netherlands 1955-1974.

	Inflation[1]	Inflation (smoothed average)	Aggressive crime[2] (p. 100.000)	Property crime[2] (p. 100.000)	Suicide[3] (p. 100.000)	Homicide[4] (p. 100.000)	Divorce[5] (p. 100.000)
1955	2.3	3.0	163.7	592	65.6	2.8	509
56	2.7	3.3	165.8	612	66.1	1.6	504
57	5.4	2.6	167.0	713	68.9	3.2	481
58	1.6	2.6	165.4	757	73.6	3.2	467
59	1.3	2.6	173.8	723	74.1	3.3	485
60	2.4	2.0	176.8	751	71.6	3.0	489
61	2.3	2.4	167.6	781	69.7	3.6	488
62	2.6	3.5	161.9	856	72.7	2.4	480
63	3.8	3.9	159.5	863	67.6	3.8	488
64	6.8	4.5	165.5	933	71.0	3.9	508
65	4.0	4.6	167.0	976	75.0	3.3	500
66	5.4	4.3	179.0	1032	77.3	4.1	544
67	3.0	4.2	178.0	1073	68.1	4.3	588
68	2.6	4.3	179.7	1167	71.0	4.0	636
69	6.3	4.9	193.2	1314	79.0	5.1	698
70	4.5	6.0	195.5	1473	88.4	4.7	788
71	8.1	7.2	202.5	1741	91.4	5.6	870
72	8.5	8.3	222.3	1977	91.0	5.4	1115
73	9.0	9.5	255.1	2210	92.7	6.0	1326

1. Consumer prices, Centraal Economisch Plan 1974.
2. C.B.S. Maandstatistiek van Politie en Justitie.
3. C.B.S. Statistisch Zakboek.
4. C.B.S. Afdeling Volksgezondheid.
5. C.B.S. Statistisch Zakboek.

Table 1b. Correlation matrix inflation (smoothed average) - anomie-indicators the Netherlands 1955-1974.

	Inflation (smoothed average)	Aggressive crime	Property crime	Suicide	Homicide	Divorce
Inflation (smoothed average)	1.00					
Aggressive crime	.89	1.00				
Property crime	.97	.94	1.00			
Suicide	.87	.87	.92	1.00		
Homicide	.83	.82	.90	.81	1.00	
Divorce	.94	.98	.96	.87	.82	1.00

Table 1c. Correlation matrix inflation - anomie-indicators the Netherlands 1955-1974.

	Inflation	Aggressive crime	Property crime	Suicide	Homicide	Divorce
Inflation	1.00					
Aggressive crime	.75	1.00				
Property crime	.82	.94	1.00			
Suicide	.75	.87	.92	1.00		
Homicide	.78	.82	.90	.81	1.00	
Divorce	.77	.98	.96	.87	.81	1.00

information about the following anomie-indicators:[39] aggressive (violent) crime, property crime, suicide,[40] homicide and divorce.

The figures of inflation for both countries refer to the increase in prices of private consumption. Sometimes changes in economic policy have disturbed the general trend of inflation. Thus the wage explosion in 1964 in the Netherlands caused a considerable increase in prices, because the central wage policy had been abandoned. That there is no such discontinuity in the trend of the anomie figures of round 1964 will stand to reason. In order to distribute the effects of such events on the rate of inflation more evenly, the smoothed average for each year has been computed on a five years basis. Both the smoothed and the uncorrected inflation figures have been correlated with the data on anomie.

Compared with the United States inflation in Holland is relatively strongly influenced by fluctuations in the level of import-prices. The average import-quota in Holland amounts to over 50%, whereas the inflation in the States should be chiefly imputed to interior causes. It goes without saying that the anomie-indicators refer exclusively to the internal situation. For this reason one would expect the correlation between anomie and inflation in the U.S. to be higher than in Holland.

Our results so far give rise to the following remarks:

39. Quantifying social conflicts, protests movements, the consumption of psychopharmaca etc. would require much more extensive research.

40. The suicide figures may be somewhat unreliable. This is due to the difficulties encountered in establishing suicide as the cause of death and to the fact that the relatives prefer to keep silent on the subject.

Table 2a. Inflation (incl. smoothed average) and anomie-indicators United States 1960-1974.

	Inflation[1]	Inflation (smoothed average)	Violent[2] Crime (p. 100.000)	Property[3] Crime (p. 100.000)	Suicide[3] (p. 100.000)	Homicide[3] (p. 100.000)	Divorce[3] (p. 1000 married women)
1960	1.6	1.10	159	946	10.6	4.7	9.2
61	1.0	1.14	156	982	10.4	4.7	9.6
62	1.1	1.24	161	1031	10.9	4.9	9.4
63	1.2	1.26	166	1126	11.0	4.9	9.6
64	1.3	1.64	188	1252	10.8	5.1	10.0
65	1.7	1.88	198	1314	11.1	5.5	10.6
66	2.9	2.60	217	1449	10.9	5.9	10.9
67	2.9	3.42	250	1672	10.8	6.8	11.2
68	4.2	4.26	295	1940	10.7	7.3	12.4
69	5.4	4.54	324	2153	11.1	7.7	13.4
70	5.9	4.62	360	2381	11.6	8.3	14.9
71	4.3	5.02	393	2514	11.7	9.1	15.7
72	3.3	5.92	398	2432	12.0	9.5	16.9
73	6.2	6.80	415	2476	12.0	9.8	18.6

1. Consumer prices, Statistical Abstracts O.E.C.D. Economic Surveys United States.
2. Uniform Crime Reports for the U.S., Statistical Abstracts.
3. Vital Statistics of the U.S., Statistical Abstracts.

Table 2b. Correlation matrix inflation (smoothed average) - anomie-indicators United States 1960-1974.

	Inflation (smoothed average	Violent crime	Property crime	Suicide	Homicide	Divorce
Inflation (smoothed average)	1.00					
Violent crime	.98	1.00				
Property crime	.98	.99	1.00			
Suicide	.76	.82	.80	1.00		
Homicide	.99	.99	.99	.83	1.00	
Divorce	.96	.99	.97	.88	.99	1.00

Table 2c. Correlation matrix inflation - anomie-indicators United States 1960-1974.

Inflation	1.00					
Violent crime	.85	1.00				
Property crime	.89	.99	1.00			
Suicide	.55	.82	.80	1.00		
Homicide	.83	.99	.99	.83	1.00	
Divorce	.78	.99	.97	.88	.99	1.00
	Inflation	Violent crime	Property crime	Suicide	Homicide	Divorce

– The results do not refute the anomie-inflation hypothesis. Far-reaching conclusions, however, cannot be drawn. The inflation percentages as well as the anomie-indicators exhibit a progressively ascending trend. For this reason the relatively high correlation coefficients cannot be trusted. Fluctuating series of figures would have furnished evidence of a more conclusive nature.
– Except in the case of suicide and inflation, the correlation in the United States are indeed higher than in Holland. This result corresponds to what has been noted above. The low suicide correlation in the U.S. might have to do with the unreliability of the statistical evidence on suicide.
– On the average, the correlations between anomie and the uncorrected figures of inflation are 0.14 lower than those between anomie and the smoothed averages. Even then the correlations are high enough not to refute our hypothesis.

The obtained results do not justify any statements of a more general nature. The correlations hold true for two countries only. In order to offer more support to our hypothesis, other countries should be taken into consideration.

Inspection of the correlation matrices of the Netherlands and the U.S.A. shows a remarkably high multi-collinearity between each of the anomie-indicators. Therefore it is permitted to reduce the number of indicators for other countries to only one. For an obvious reason preference has been given to the divorce-indicator: in many countries the statistics for the other indicators (except suicide) are either differently

Table 3. Inflation (smoothed average) and Anomie (divorce, 1956 = 100) 1956-1974 for selected countries.

	Netherlands		U.S.A.		England		Sweden		Norway		W. Germany	
	I	A	I	A	I	A	I	A	I	A	I	A
1956	3.38	100	1.54	100	3.52	100	3.46	100	3.38	100	1.78	100
1957	2.66	94	1.66	98	3.40	90	3.22	104	2.90	98	1.98	100
1958	2.86	92	2.00	95	2.66	86	3.66	101	2.90	100	1.80	100
1959	2.86	94	1.92	99	2.36	93	3.38	103	2.64	105	1.78	101
1960	1.94	96	1.48	98	2.46	92	3.32	106	3.28	112	1.98	101
1961	2.14	96	1.18	102	2.26	97	2.84	103	2.60	117	2.14	102
1962	3.08	96	1.26	100	2.80	111	3.52	106	3.28	116	2.40	103
1963	3.46	96	1.30	102	3.54	123	3.60	101	4.14	116	2.82	105
1964	4.38	101	1.66	106	3.64	134	4.44	110	4.14	122	3.04	110
1965	4.64	100	1.98	113	3.28	147	4.44	114	3.94	123	2.74	116
1966	4.76	108	2.58	116	3.82	151	4.20	122	4.24	128	2.50	114
1967	5.10	117	3.42	119	4.24	167	4.06	126	3.72	137	2.58	122
1968	4.94	125	4.26	132	4.58	177	4.46	131	4.98	145	2.66	126
1969	5.32	136	4.54	143	5.68	197	4.66	141	5.54	148	3.00	138
1970	6.20	153	4.64	159	6.60	222	4.98	150	6.10	161	3.80	147
1971	7.06	168	5.04	167	7.50	281	5.94	158	6.90	173	4.82	152
1972	7.48	219	6.14	180	9.64	415	8.16	180	8.24	186	5.68	163
1973	8.64	264	6.80	195	13.22	392	8.60	196	8.50	212	6.12	169

Sources: Economic Survey of Europe, 1970-1974.
Population, 1975, p. 1004.

classified or unavailable. Even the divorce data can only be used as an index of anomie in a limited number of countries. Particularly in catholic countries, these figures are not reliable, on account of the large number of 'hidden' divorces.

Our further research has been restricted to the following non-catholic countries: Holland, U.S.A., England, Sweden, Norway and West-Germany. The collected data refer to inflation (smoothed average on a five year basis) and divorce (in order to eliminate unitial differences between the countries: 1956 = 100) for the period 1956-1974 (table 3). The computed regression equations and correlations for the various countries are presented in figure 1. The correlation between anomie and inflation varies between 0.88 and 0.96 (the t-values are satisfactory); the regression equations are located in the same area of the diagram. The resulting anomie-inflation equation for all six countries runs as follows:

$$I = 0.034\ A - 0.4330 \qquad R = 0.86$$
$$(17.61)$$

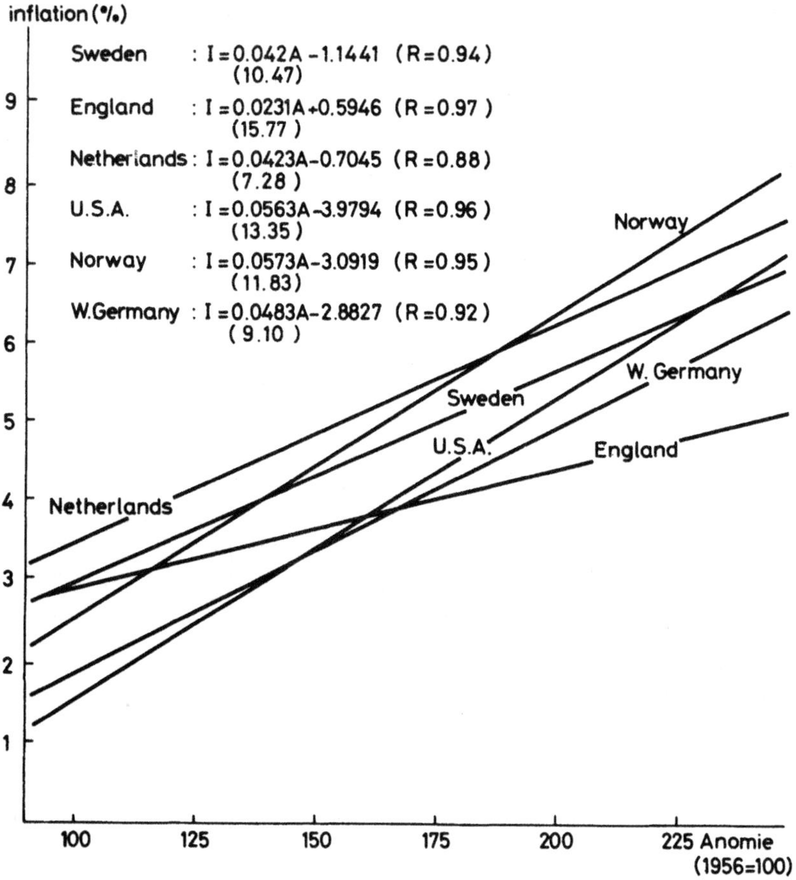

Figure 1. Regression equations and correlation coefficients R (t-values), anomie and inflation 1956-1974, selected countries.

Finally, the figures in table 3 have been used for a modest cross-section analysis. In accordance with our hypothesis countries with a relatively high rate of inflation should also score high on the degree of anomie, and vice versa. This indeed appears to be the case. In England with its high inflation, anomie is also higher than in all other countries. Another typical example is Germany where both inflation and anomie are lower than elsewhere. The cross-section correlation computed for the year 1973 (six countries) yields the following results:

$$I = 0.029\ A + 1.7886 \qquad R = 0.95$$
$$(6.12)$$

Summarizing our findings we may indeed conclude that there is a significant relation between the degree of anomie and the rate of inflation in society.

6.8. Evaluation

Until now anomie and inflation have been studied by two separate disciplines. In this paper these phenomena have been presented as aspects of a single accelerating process of social change. Basically, both phenomena point to a collective transgression of formerly more generally accepted restrictions of alternative modes of behaviour. From an interdisciplinary point of view current inflation is perhaps best described by terms like anomic inflation or social structural inflation.

A continuation of the exponential rise of the rate of inflation (and of the anomie-indicators) in the future is hardly conceivable. The extrapolation of recent developments implies total economic and social disruption within a few years.

Besides deepening our understanding, an interdisciplinary approach should ideally lead to additional policy proposals. This paper doesn't offer the firm grounds on which such proposals should be based. Nevertheless we would like to conclude with a few tentative remarks.

If we accept the assumed relation between anomie and inflation, a decline in the anomie-indicators will simultaneously imply a decline in the rate of inflation. Integration is inversely related to inflation. Policy instruments which check anomie will at the same time combat inflation.

Furthering integration in a modern pluralistic society is no simple matter. The advancing individualization restricts the policy alternatives. Solutions derived from the pre-industrial past do not apply. Once, obedience to church, king and state afforded moral security and a sense of belonging. For modern society such a system of behaviour control by universally accepted normative codes must be regarded as a form of collective regression.

The same goes for conformism imposed by means of a law and order policy. It may be that anomie is temporarily suppressed; at the same time, however, such a policy provokes potential conflicts, as the requisite reforms are obstructed.

Although the possibilities of integration on macro-level may be limited in a democratic society, a future-orientated policy might stand the best chance of succeeding. Policy-planning backed by scientific research into processes of social change is still in its infancy. The foundation in Holland of the 'Sociaal Cultureel Planbureau' besides the 'Centraal Planbureau' is a step in the right direction.

The specific nature of modern society being given, there would perhaps be more sense in fighting anomie on meso- and micro-level. Integrated and relatively autonomous subgroups – at work as well as in leisure time – contribute to the normative control of impulses, even when consensus on macro-level is absent. Minimizing conflicts between these groups, however, remains a problem. Extending institutionalized consultation might help in canalizing these conflicts. Anomie calls for highly developed systems of conflict-management.

At this stage a further specification of potential policy instruments is not yet possible. For the present our objective has been achieved if this paper gives an impetus to further research into the relation between anomie and inflation, or, more generally, if it stimulates the cooperation between sociologists and economists,

7. Impressions of a symposium

Adam Szirmai

During the two days of the symposium *Economics and Sociology, Towards an Integration,* economists and sociologists engaged in intensive discussions of the issues raised in the papers presented here. More than the papers, it is these discussions that illustrate how the interaction between economists and sociologists proceeds in practice. In this personally tinged account I shall endeavour to give an impression of these discussions and of the general atmosphere at the symposium.

7.1. Smelser on rationality and economic stagnation

The first speaker is Professor N.J. Smelser from Berkeley. As an economic sociologist he has become known through publications such as *Economy and Society* (with Parsons)[1] and the introductory handbook *The Sociology of Economic Life*[2]. At the time of the symposium he was engaged on a revision of this handbook, of which the second edition has meanwhile been published. Themes from the book such as the analysis of economic rationality and the social consequences of economic change, reappear in his symposium paper, *On the Relevance of Economic Sociology for Economics.* It is worthwhile noting that in the book Smelser writes about the social consequences of economic growth, while in the paper he concentrates on the more topical problems of economic stagnation.

Smelser gives a short summary of his paper. He is a good speaker, quiet and self-assured. Evidently while speaking he can shake off the doubts and uncertainties to which his subject doubtless gives rise, for him too.

1. T. Parsons and N.J. Smelser, *Economy and Society,* London, 1965.
2. N.J. Smelser, *The Sociology of Economic Life,* Englewood Cliffs, N.J. Prentice Hall 1963.

According to Smelser, a rather simplistic concept of rationality is used in economic models: consumers and producers choose rationally in order to optimize their economic position. Sociologists see economic rationality as one of the many possible institutionalized values. This opens the way for a discussion of the manner in which a series of non-economic 'rationalities' influence economic actions. From Economic Anthropology we can learn that market exchange, as we know it, is only one of the possible types of exchange. Patterns of exchange are often determined by traditional values, whereby loose principles of reciprocity play a part. Other kinds of exchange are redistributive by nature. Also, the amount of calculation in the several types of exchange can vary. For instance within close kinship relationships there is usually less calculation. Smelser next refers to studies of communist and socialist economies, in which markets play a subordinate role. Here economic exchanges are strongly influenced by 'political rationalities'. The same applies to the economic activities of the very large corporations in the West. Finally, Smelser points to the growing importance of the 'grants economy' whereby non-economic rationalities increasingly influence the distribution of economic goods and services. Referring to the ideal-type approach of Weber, Smelser advocates the development of models of economic action 'that incorporate or synthesize a number of single models of rationality in different combinations'.[3] He has little faith in the approach of the institutionalists (see Kapp and Gruchy). They develop in an antitheoretical direction, concentrating on institutional description. He also criticizes the exchange-theorists for: 'taking over the formal apparatus of economics and emptying it of content'.

We know little about the consequences of economic stagnation. Such studies as exist on social and economic change relate to growth processes. Nevertheless, Smelser hazards a number of speculations. In general it may be said that the processes of social differentiation characteristic for growth, will not be reversed in the event of stagnation. 'We are left with an institutional excess capacity'. The economic consequences of stagnation will be 'regressive', will weigh the heaviest on the weakest shoulders. 'Non-productive' welfare activities such as education, medicine and social services will be threatened.

The materialistic status symbolization that characterizes our social stratification may change as energy and resources become scarcer. Class

3. N.J. Smelser, The Relevance of Economic Sociology for Economics, p. 13.

struggle will become defensive and grim, aimed at maintaining secured positions. The chances of upward social mobility for the bottommost groups will disappear.[4]

Cultural values will also be strongly affected by stagnation. Values indicated by the term 'Protestant ethic' – freedom to exploit the natural environment, the ethos of work, control, achievement, ambition, rationality in economic and social life – may be questioned. Possibly more 'humanistic' value systems will become functional in circumstances of stagnation.

Finally, political tensions will increase. Democracies will be threatened. In any event, a greater degree of collectivization of goods, services and natural resources may be expected.

The co-referent Professor C. de Galan[5] feels that Smelser has made a valuable contribution. He has indicated how economic sociology can supplement economics. Thus, there are several fields where Western economics hardly applies, f.i. relationships within the family, social insurance, or life in simple communities. In many cases the assumptions of economics are too simplistic. Data that are not easily quantifiable are often left out of consideration. Where policy is concerned economics – an aspect science – does in fact need supplementing by other social sciences.

However – as de Galan quite rightly stresses – it is easier to defend the need for integration than to realize it. Potentially economic sociology is useful for economists. But Smelser's speculations on stagnation have not yet convinced De Galan of its actual usefulness at this moment.

De Galan would like to structure the discussion to some extent. If we ever want to achieve integration, the 'demand' of economists and the 'supply' of sociologists will have to be adjusted to one another. He asks sociologists: what is economic sociology? What can it contribute by way of knowledge and insight? In what ways is it relevant for economists? He quizzes economists. What do you ask from economic sociology? What are the weak points of economics? In this context De Galan himself mentions: 1. consumer behaviour. What does rational consumer behaviour entail? How do consumers' scales of preference shift? 2. Inflation theory. 3. Labour market theory.

The plenary discussion on 'rationality' is heated and rather confused.

4. Cf. R.L. Heilbroner, *An Inquiry into the Human Prospect*, New York, Norton, 1974.

5. Professor of Labour Economics at Groningen University.

The general feeling is that Smelser should not have spoken of different kinds of rationality or of the subordination of one kind of rationality to another. Various alternative formulations are suggested: 'different backgrounds to rationality', 'different calculation attitudes', 'different constraints under which one maximizes in equilibrium or disequilibrium situations', 'different values'. Smelser's conclusion: 'When academics discuss rationality they usually become very emotional' is not unjustified. Ultimately nobody disagrees with the proposition that in some exchange relations there is more calculation than in others and that in different kinds of exchange different value systems play a part.

The discussion is not very satisfactory. It remains at too high a level of abstraction. What one hopes for are concrete examples of how one could improve on the results of economic research by using other theoretical models. But, as so often in sociology, Smelser gets no further than listing a series of factors that ought to be taken into account, somehow.

In the discussion about the social consequences of economic stagnation several of the economists present express their distrust of sociological crystal gazing. 'No need for doomsday prophecy'. The Groningen economist Kuipers denies that there is a shortage of natural resources in the technical sense. According to him, stagnation is not inevitable. Smelser admits that his assumptions are pessimistic. However, he is of the opinion that speculations like his can stimulate the search for new ways of exploiting scarce natural resources. One should not rule out the already existing antagonism to further exploitation of resources. Think of environmentalism and anti-modernism. Kapp adds that resources are definitely scarce, both economically and technically. Beyond a certain point it costs more energy to get raw materials out of the ground than the energy gained in the process. Geyer points to an interesting paradox in Smelser's thinking. On the one hand the latter sees a threat to democratic values, and on the other he hopes for a 'humanistic resurgence'. Smelser stresses the need for studies of specific historical situations and societies. He can not give a general answer. Blau denies that there is a paradox: 'In the Middle Ages humanistic values existed alongside with extremely authoritarian political arrangements'.

A lively discussion develops on what economics 'demands' from sociologists. According to the Utrecht professor of economics Brenner the motivations connected with processes of economic growth no longer seem to work. He asks sociologists to study economic motivations. 'What new motivations could motivate economic activities, now that fear of starvation and acquisitiveness, the older motivations of capitalism, are diminishing?' Gadourek replies that sociologists have done much survey research on problems of job motivation, attitudes towards work and leisure, value patterns, etc... According to Gadourek, sociologists can aid economists in several ways: 1. by empirically examining specific variables from economics, e.g. the propensity to consume, 2. by introducing sociological variables into the analysis of economic processes and 3. by interpreting economic phenomena as institutions and studying them as such, e.g. the labour market. Simons indicates how sociologists could improve economic models by studying the conditions in which rational calculation occurs: 'the notion of bounded rationality'. Huppes argues that the economists' conception of reality is an equilibrium conception. In periods of social disequilibrium they need sociological variables more than ever.

In these discussions economists and sociologists are carefully feeling each other out. To a certain extent, this is a one-way process. It is the potential contribution of sociology that is being discussed, more than that of economics. As soon as the discussion becomes somewhat more general, the economists tend to withdraw into their falsifiable models. Sociologists make series of interesting suggestions, without becoming very concrete. Not for the first time I find it rather disappointing that discussions by specialists in the social sciences on extremely important themes like the social consequences of economic stagnation, do not yield much more than random conversations between non-specialized intellectuals.

7.2. Institutionalists

In their lectures Kapp and Gruchy deal with the contributions of institutional economics. Gruchy once defined institutionalism as follows: 'The study of the structure and functioning of the evolving field of human relations which is concerned with the provision of material goods and services for the satisfaction of human wants... it is the study of the changing patterns of cultural relations which deal with the creation and disposal of scarce material goods and services by individuals and groups in the light of their private and public aims'.[6]

6. A.G. Gruchy, *Modern Economic Thought, The American Contribution,* New York, Prentice Hall, 1947, pp. 550-552.

It is an approach that fits in well with the developmental perspective in sociology.[7] Consequently various authors known as institutionalists may also be found in sociological bibliographies: Veblen, Heilbroner, Galbraith, Myrdal and so on. However, it turns out that the work of such authors can better be understood against the background of a lengthy polemic within economics, a polemic in which the controversy also known in sociology between advocates of empirical precision and systematic theory and advocates of scope and relevance, plays an important part.[8]

7.3. Circular interdependencies within a process of cumulative causation

K.W. Kapp is an American economist by origin who has worked and published on the environmental consequences of economic growth, long before the subject became popular. In 1968 he wrote an article entitled '*In Defense of Institutional Economics*'[9] which has become wellknown in the meanwhile. In his contribution to the symposium, *In Defense of Institutionalism,* he has elaborated on the themes of the earlier article supplementing it with new material. Kapp is an inspiring speaker. He gives the impression of having much more to tell than he can possibly pass on in the limited time allotted to him. In any case he has a stimulating and provocative effect on his audience. Kapp polemizes against the orthodox neo-classical mainstream in economics. Orthodox economists isolate economic processes in closed systems. Their highly formal analytical and mathematical approach leads to much too strong a distinction between the 'economic' and the 'non-economic'. Their attitude towards an interdisciplinary approach is negative. In their

7. See J. Goudsblom, *Balans van de Sociologie,* Utrecht, Aula, 1974, pp. 87-128. N. Elias, *Was ist Soziologie?,* München, Juventa Verlag, 1970, pp. 168-195.
8. For these terms see J. Goudsblom, op. cit. 1974. In this book Goudsblom gives a birdeye's view of the development of sociology. According to Goudsblom different approaches and schools in sociology stress different scientific ideals and criteria. He distinguishes four general ideals: empirical precision, systematic theory, scope and relevance. These ideals often conflict with each other. Goudsblom especially stresses the tension between precision and 'systematics' on the one hand and scope and relevance on the other.
9. K.W. Kapp, In Defense of Institutional Economics, in *Swedish Journal of Economics,* March 1968, pp. 1-18.

atomistic view of society economic processes always tend towards an equilibrium. Mechanical analogies prevail in their thinking.

In contrast with this, institutionalists study economic processes as open systems in dynamic interaction with more comprehensive political and social systems and in interaction with natural systems. For instance orthodox economists have neglected environmental problems. Here Kapp advocates the idea of irreversible exchange relations between the economic system and the natural system. Natural resources and energy, the inputs of the economic system, are converted into outputs of waste and pollution.

Unlike the orthodox economists, the institutionalists are interested in longterm evolutionary processes: development processes in the industrial societies and development processes in the Third World. In this context they have a special interest in the role of science and technology, in the part played by power relationships and by conflicting interests.

Kapp does not agree with Smelser that the institutionalists are a-theoretical. With the by now obligatory reference to Kuhn he is of the opinion that the institutionalists have a new 'disciplinary matrix' that offers an alternative to the equilibrium model of traditional economics. He is referring to the 'principle of circular interlocking interdependencies within a process of cumulative causation' developed by Myrdal. In this model there is no more place for final causes. In social development processes there are countless interconnected factors that influence and react on one another. Kapp illustrates this by means of a series of interconnected variables, taken from Myrdal's *Asian Drama,* which play a part in the process of development – or rather the absence thereof – in the Third World: productivity per capita, conditions of production, levels of living, attitudes towards production, work and living, various institutions, policies and legislation.

Social processes do not tend towards an equilibrium; they reinforce themselves, they are cumulative: gaps between rich and poor are widening, economic growth is exponential, economic depressions are intensifying themselves, social conflicts are escalating. Active intervention in social processes is necessary. One can no longer believe that in the long run laissez-faire will lead to an acceptable equilibrium.

Kapp concludes with an impassioned plea for transdisciplinary work, in which the boundaries of disciplines are systematically transcended: 'the era of integration is starting now'.

In the discussion it is mainly economists who enter the lists this time.

The co-referent Nentjes reproaches Kapp for sketching a caricature of neo-classical economics. The analytical instruments of neo-classical thought can be utilized for the study of many phenomena besides equilibrium phenomena. Nentjes himself, for instance, is aiming at a neo-classical analysis of environmental problems.

It is questioned whether institutionalism does in fact form a paradigm. Kapp mentions several variables that should be taken into account in research, but he doesn't formulate systematic theoretical connections between these variables. Kapp doubts whether our mathematical instruments are suitable for the study of development processes but – as Nentjes puts it – 'If one has many variables and no quantification, then the system becomes indeterminate'. Others argue that though the principles formulated by Kapp and Myrdal form part of a disciplinary matrix, they do not form a complete matrix.

The contrasts between different types of economists are clearly marked when the discussion centers on falsifiability. The mathematically oriented economists Kuipers and Muysken challenge Kapp to mention one clearly falsifiable hypothesis that an ordinary economist could not formulate. Muysken in turn is immediately attacked by Schenk, a business economist: the predictions of economists and econometricians are not all that good, in spite of the objective air with which they are often presented. Muysken: 'I can make predictions, even though they are wrong'. A caricature of this position is offered by Derksen from Utrecht: 'Classical economics has general, universal propositions. This is the mark of real science. Institutionalism is not a real science'.

Kapp replies with an attack on the pseudo-precision of the economists. For instance, the usual cost-benefit analysis does not make the slightest allowance for the wants of those who cannot pay for certain goods or services. Even if they are not presented in a mathematical form, studies by institutionalists do end up in policy proposals. Policy then forms a test of the theories. As an example of a falsifiable prediction Kapp mentions the failure of the green revolution. The institutionalists had predicted this failure since factors like patterns of land ownership and power relationships had been ignored.

Repeatedly the question is raised what institutionalism really is and what subjects would be taught as such. People are especially dissatisfied with Kapp's refusal to demarcate his discipline: 'follow the problem'. Kuipers, the most prominent representative of the mathematically oriented economists, asks in an aggressive tone whether anyone can give him a clear definition of institutionalism in a few sentences. In the present undefined form he has no need for Institutional Economics. The relationship between institutional and orthodox economics is also unclear. (Members of the public express their agreement with these sentiments).

Some try to give Kuipers an answer, e.g. Huppes: 'Institutionalists study the influence of institutional structures on economic processes'. This is not very satisfactory. Unlike many economic theories, institutionalism cannot be summarized in a few sentences or formulas. It is a historical and situational approach. If a study like *Asian Drama* is summarized in a few sentences, it becomes meaningless. In my opinion Kapp contributed precisely to this misunderstanding by presenting institutionalism by means of the rather abstract principle of interlocking interdependencies etc. and by means of a list of 'variables', instead of presenting substantive examples more extensively. Incidentally, it is striking that both Gruchy and Kapp use a system language which in sociology is associated with more static, less historical ways of practising science.

Towards the end of the discussion Brenner addresses himself sarcastically to those who are so keen to immunize themselves against institutionalism by labelling it 'unscientific'. Is it more unscientific to try to determine the direction of a stream of molecules than the movements of the seperate molecules themselves, he asks. 'Once can use neo-classical economics for the analysis of the problems of capitalism and institutional economics for the problems of the development of capitalism'. Kapp himself is in no way disconcerted by all the criticism: 'In our knowledge of economic processes we are on the verge of a ptolemaeic revolution. A new paradigm is on the horizon'.

7.4. Institutional versus orthodox economics

On the second day of the symposium Professor Gruchy presents a paper entitled *Institutional vs. Orthodox Economics and the Interdisciplinary Approach.* In his career A.G. Gruchy has made it his particular task to publicize the ideas of original institutionalists. In 1947 he gave a summary of prewar institutionalism in *Modern Economic Thought.*[10] In

10. A.G. Gruchy, op. cit., 1947.

1958 he helped found the Association for Evolutionary Economics and in 1972 he published *Contemporary Economic Thought,* in which he discussed the work of postwar institutionalists such as Ayres, Galbraith, Myrdal and Colm.[11] His lecture can also be characterized as a summary of a series of books and ideas. There is quite a lot of overlap with the contribution of Kapp. Gruchy also emphasizes the dynamic and open-system character of institutionalism and the fact that institutionalists study the development of economics within the framework of larger social wholes. Thanks to their openness, institutionalists are especially suited for cooperation with representatives of other social sciences. For instance, very clear parallels can be drawn between institutionalism and macro-sociology as practised by people like Daniel Bell.

The development of science and of technology are factors of the greatest importance for the institutionalists. Although they are not determinists, they see a 'logic of economic development'. In industrial societies the logic of economic development leads to a 'logic of reform': a coordination of economic processes by national planning and national consultative structures.

At the end of his talk Gruchy gives a sketch of what the teaching of institutional economics would have to entail. He would begin by comparing his definition of institutional economics (see p.164) with orthodox definitions. Next the students would have to acquaint themselves with the theory of culture. The third phase would be concerned with the study of industrialism and of the development of the industrial system. Then the emphasis would shift to the modern tripartite industrial economy, with its market system, its planning system and its public sector. The final stage would be an analysis of future developments, of the logic of reform. As part of this, a systematic study would be made of planning experiences in various countries.

Strangely enough, this rather uninspiring contribution is received much more kindly and less aggressively by the economists than that of Kapp. True, the co-referent, Kuipers, begins his comments on a critical note: orthodox economics has been given a distorted presentation by Gruchy. For instance it is not correct that dynamic studies and theories do not exist. Think of examples such as studies of trade cycles or economic growth. There is no point in listing a series of problems that

11. A.G. Gruchy, *Contemporary Economic Thought. The Contribution of neo-institutional Economics,* London, MacMillan, 1972.

economists cannot solve, thus writing off economics. You have to look at the problems that can be explained by economics.[12] In this context Kuipers mentions price determination, allocation of means of production, income distribution, international trade and unemployment. (In my opinion all of them subjects for which a purely economic approach is inadequate).

However, after an aggressive start Kuipers begins to speak more softly and hesitantly. In a rather dramatic atmosphere he states that he has now understood what institutionalism is about. Institutionalists try to obtain a general picture of the development of economic systems. They study the interactions between technology and economic processes, between cultural systems and economic systems. Such problems have indeed been neglected by economists and econometricians. Kuipers admits that he sees a place for such a subject in an economic faculty. However, one should realize that the institutionalist approach is very broad and somewhat superficial. There are also more specific problems which need to be tackled more technically, in depth. We should try to develop forms of cooperation within our department. Incidentally, Kuipers, now speaking more fiercely, is of the opinion that the various logics – logic of economic development, of cultural development, of reform – have not been underbuilt thoroughly enough.

In an extensive discussion of the relation between technology and economic development it is posited that the institutionalists demonstrate the need for studies of this relationship but continue to work too programmatically. Galbraith for instance, has developed the rudiments of a theory of technology,[13] but it has not been elaborated very much. Jacobs advises Gruchy to take a look at the literature of applied economics, where people like Marris, Wood, Eatwell and others try to define technology. Gadourek referres to the countless sociological studies in the tradition of Ogburn.

Gruchy admits that the institutionalists work rather programmatically.

12. A similar discussion is that between the institutionalist Heilbroner and the neo-classical economist Solow. Heilbroner stresses the great social problems of our time and concludes that economics is irrelevant. Solow emphasizes theoretical relevance, mentions a series of problems that economics *can* explain and argues that these insights acquired by economists *may* be relevant for *some* social problems. See Heilbroner, 'On the limited "Relevance" of Economics', and Solow, 'Science and Ideology in Economics', in Bell and Kristol, *Capitalism Today,* New York, London, Basic Books, 1972.

13. See Galbraith, *The New Industrial State,* New York, Signet 1968 and *Economics and the Public Purpose,* New York, Signet 1975.

He attributes this to their marginal and defensive position in the academic world. The discussion ends on a note of conciliation. The institutionalists admit the utility of orthodox model-building and theorizing, and the economists advocate cooperation with institutionalists and even sociologists. A felicitous but rather surprising development, which should be attributed to processes of group dynamics, rather than to the high level and clarity of the discussions.

7.5. Anomie and inflation

Unlike the previous speakers, the Groningen economist/sociologist Huppes tries to show how economics and sociology can be integrated by means of a concrete theme. This makes his paper *Anomie and Inflation* one of the most vulnerable but at the same time one of the most interesting contributions to the symposium. His point of departure is, that so far economists have not been able to formulate any adequate measures against steadily increasing inflation. An interdisciplinary approach can help us further.

First of all Huppes reviews the various economic inflation theories: 1. demand-pull inflation. Too great a demand for goods and services leads to price increases (Keynes); 2. cost-push inflation. Competition on the market has been disturbed. Large concerns, monopolists and oligopolists can push up their prices. Unions, monopolists on the labour market, can cause wage costs to rise. A wage-price spiral is created. A special variant of the cost-push inflation theories is Levinson's. He explains price inflation by the efforts of the large concerns to maximize their cash flow; 3. monetary inflation. The government and the banks put too much money into circulation. In the final instance all forms of inflation may be regarded as disturbances of a (market) equilibrium situation, in which various groups – entrepreneurs, consumers, workers, government – try to improve their position in respect of other groups.

Inflation is typically a phenomenon of disequilibrium. Economic explanations are inadequate because economists think too much in terms of equilibrium. This applies even to Keynesian theory.[14] Economists are

14. For instance even Keynesians take the institutional structure within which economic processes run their course, as given. The authorities do not intervene directly in the economy. They take macro-economic measures, trusting that these measures will have their effect via the existing market relations.

coming to the conclusion that the behaviour of various groups in society is irrational from the economic point of view. The question they do not ask is: why has such a lack of collective self-control developed?

In recent years critics within the discipline of sociology have been arguing that their discipline has been much too static and harmonious. Huppes, however, believes that as compared to economics, sociology has comparative advantages in explaining disequilibrium and conflict. The sociological tradition of the study of anomie can contribute to the explanation of inflation. In this context Huppes successively discusses the well-known anomie concepts of Durkheim and Merton.

In an earlier article Huppes has given an outline of an interdisciplinary perspective based on the exchange theory.[15] He suggests that prices can be regarded as norms, market mechanisms as forms of social control and income distribution as the distribution of power. Inflation can now be interpreted as a process in which collective norms lose their influence. Inflation and anomie are linked. Unfortunately Huppes does not make it quite clear, how he thinks the phenomena are exactly related. The most probable interpretation is that inflation is one of the various forms of anomie. Sociological explanations of anomie will at the same time be explanations of inflation. Both inflation and other forms of anomie are bound up with the uncertainty that arises in periods of rapid social change, the chief cause of which is the acceleration of the technological development.

At the end of his paper Huppes tries to test the connection between anomie and inflation empirically. As indicators of anomie he chooses aggressive crimes, property crimes, suicides, murders and divorces. For the Netherlands over the 1955-1973 period and for the United States over the 1960-1972 period the figures for these indicators are correlated with the inflation rates. Reasonably high correlations result. Huppes concludes that his hypothesis is not refuted. To strengthen the hypothesis further research is necessary.

The co-referents Groenveld and Wilpstra are rather critical. Once again Huppes has drawn a caricature of economics. Exchange theory, they assert, has the same drawbacks as neo-classical economics: both approaches are tautological. The theoretical connection between anomie and inflation has not been precisely formulated. If you correlate time series in a period in which everything is going up, you always get high

15. T. Huppes, Economic Sociology or Sociological Economics, see chapter 2.

correlations. They wonder whether Huppes' contribution is anything more than 'a brilliant play of words'.

Although some of the economists present share the scepticism of the co-referents, in general one is grateful to Huppes for having ventured on a substantive study. Brenner in particular agrees with Huppes, arguing that historical research has shown that rapid social changes were always accompanied by inflation.

Critical comments broadly follow those of Groenveld and Wilpstra. General correlations of time series do not tell us very much (Kuipers). What exactly are the causal relations between the various indicators of anomie and inflation (Kuipers, Korver, Muysken)? There is also some quite justified criticism of the choice of indicators. For instance can one automatically say that divorce is an indicator of anomie (Korver)? Did not Durkheim distinguish between different kinds of suicide? Each indicator is a composite index which implies that the differences between various groups *within* the countries chosen, are neglected (Ellemers).

Smelser is of the opinion that Huppes has made a valuable contribution. But, social breakdown, though important, is not the sole cause of inflation. He suggests that it might be worthwile to look at wage differentials and relative deprivation. He advocates a more historical and comparative approach. The degree of effectiveness or ineffectiveness of the political system might also be an important factor, independently of the degree of anomie in society (see Britain for instance).

In his reply Huppes stresses that his research is still in a preliminary stage. His main concern was to show how economists and sociologists can meaningfully cooperate.

Much of the criticism that came to the fore in the discussion can be traced to Huppes' loose, associative style. He ought to argue his choice of indicators far more extensively and systematically. The hypothesis and the theoretical relationships should be formulated much more strictly. I have in mind here for instance the in itself illuminating analogy between prices and norms. Further, it is clear that exchange theory has served as a source of inspiration for Huppes. But the anomie-inflation hypothesis can be presented just as well without referring to exchange theory.

The main criticism lies in the question whether one ought not rather interpret inflation as a social conflict than as anomie. Admittedly, conflicts between groups in society imply that common norms are crumbling. But within the conflicting groups the members themselves can live in accordance with clearcut sets of group norms and ideologies. Is there any point in characterizing society as anomic in that case?

In my opinion *Anomie and Inflation* is the most successful attempt at integration during the symposium. The idea of thinking about inflation in sociological terms as anomie (or conflict) is a stimulating one. I have dwelt somewhat longer on this paper because it illustrates at the same time how little progress has been made towards the integration of economics and sociology. The paper begins with the remark that economic instruments against inflation are inadequate. However, as Huppes will immediately admit, the alternatives presented – a future-oriented policy, extending institutionalized consultation etc. – are very meager. Both theoretically and empirically the bulk of the work is still to be done.

7.6. Problems of validity, praxiology and positivism

As the last of the speakers I. Gadourek presents his paper *Convergence and diversification in the methodologies of Economics and Sociology.* By means of a more or less impressionistic, exploratory study of textbooks he has tried to determine to what extent there are similarities or differences in the ways economics and sociology approach their subjects of study and to what extent the disciplines are converging or diverging.

I do not feel qualified to say much about the main body of the paper, a rather technical comparison of methods of data collection and data processing. Gadourek is a typical representative of the technical-methodological subculture within sociology. It is sad but true that the channels of communication between this subculture and other subcultures within sociology have become blocked. If one wants to do studies the results of which can be tested and which are of some practical relevance for the policy of various social groups or organizations, the need for quantification is obvious. On the other hand it is doubtful whether a high degree of mathematicization is justified, as long as fundamental problems concerning the *validity* of our observations in sociology, still remain unsolved. For myself, such doubts have a highly inhibiting effect. An integration problem par excellence.

At any event Gadourek concludes that in this field there is a certain degree of convergence and exchange of techniques. Sociologists have taken over techniques like path analysis and multiple-regression analysis from economists. Economists have become more aware of qualitative variables. From psychologists and sociologists they have borrowed scale techniques and methods of factor analysis.

In the rest of the paper a number of particularly interesting contrasts are considered. One of the most intriguing propositions is, that the fundamental epistemological problems of the two disciplines are different. In sociology the main problem is that of validity – for Gadourek too. For economists one of the most important questions is, whether the models they construct are 'positive' approximations of reality or normative structures. In the normative approach, also known as the 'praxiological approach', economists devise models of what would happen *if* people were rational in their economic actions. Rational action in that case becomes a normative criterion by which actual behaviour can be appraised. 'While the main problem of economics seems to be that of reconciling the praxiologist and the positivist views, that of sociology lies in the validation of covert and overt knowledge, in reconciling the interpretative and explanatory conceptions of social science'.[16]

According to Gadourek, description, interpretation of the cultural meanings of social behaviour and classification predominate in sociology. What passes for theorizing is often no more than the construction of large classificatory schemata. In economics description, interpretation and classification play a much smaller part. The approach is hypothetical-deductive. Starting from a number of axioms, analytical models are devised to explain economic phenomena. Explanation, causal analysis and prediction are much more important than in sociology.

For economists data collection is hardly a problem. Figures are available from the balance sheets of firms, from reports of statistical institutes and planning bureaux. Economists concentrate on formulating hypothetical deductive macro-models and try to 'adapt' these to the data. Sociologists, on the other hand, have to devote a large part of their energy to collecting their data. They usually operate at micro-level by means of interviews with individuals or direct observations.

Gadourek concludes that on the whole – except for some exchanges of techniques – the disciplines are hardly converging. Though he does believe that economists and sociologists can learn much from one

16. I. Gadourek, Convergence and Diversification in the Methodologies of Economics and Sociology, p. 103.

another, Gadourek is not an advocate of disciplinary integration. On the contrary, he advocates disciplinary specialization and cooperation between the specialists. Via their techniques of data-collection sociologists can supply information useful to economists. They can encourage the inclusion of sociological variables in economic models. Finally, they can study economic institutions in the same way as they study schools, hospitals, and other social institutions.

It is a pity that Gadourek's contribution is the last one. People are beginning to get tired. Gadourek's interesting and sometimes controversial ideas deserve more attention, than they got in the discussion.

In his comment the Groningen professor of mathematical economics Pikkemaat reproaches Gadourek for not having defined the subjects of study of economics and sociology. How can one talk about convergence and diversification if these subjects are not defined in advance? Gadourek disagrees. The consensus that arises among the practitioners of a discipline with regard to their subject of study, can be studied empirically. It is not necessary to give a definition of one's own. Gadourek is not as apodictic as Pikkemaat would like him to be.

Some of the economists think that the contrast between normative economics and praxiological economics has been exaggerated. But no one seems to disagree basically with Gadourek in this respect. Others ask Gadourek what contribution the methodologist could make to interdisciplinary work. Gadourek repeats that economists and sociologists can learn from each other. However, one should not aim at the merging of the two disciplines into one big mother discipline. That would be a step backwards. The pursuit of integration may be designated – negatively – by the term 'mutual imperialism'. This also holds for the methodological field. Complete unification is neither possible nor desirable. What we need is cooperation between specialists.

7.7. Final discussion

The possibilities of integration also form the theme of the final discussion. The greatest optimists are the institutionalists, who see transdisciplinary work as something just round the corner. But in the somewhat euphoric mood at the end of the symposium almost all the speakers seem to support the idea of further integration. In a short summary Smelser tries to give his impressions of the past two days. He believes that the symposium was successful, especially because of the occurrence and reoccurrence of continuous themes. There was a 'persistent preoccupation with the issue of the limits of formal economics'. The problem is 'how to maintain some sense of theoretical integrity and at the same time to widen the scope'. Various people argue that in scientific work one should rather concentrate on problems than on disciplines. Those who want to participate in new forms of interdisciplinary organization should, however, be familiar with at least one of the traditional disciplines. Therefore the idea that the whole of university education starting from the first year should be organized in interdisciplinary fashion around problem areas, is rejected. On this note of consensus the symposium is closed.

In my opinion the symposium was worthwhile, above all on account of the discussions. On the one hand it once more became clear how difficult interdisciplinary work really is. On the other hand, a certain exchange of information and ideas was definitely realized. The willingness to talk across disciplinary boundaries was quite striking. Although the participants were seldom able to convince each other by rational argument, my impression is that mutual prejudices were weakened.

For myself the most important discovery of these two days was that the debate in sociology between advocates of empirical precision and theoretical order on the one hand and advocates of relevance and scope on the other, manifests itself in almost identical form in economics. In both disciplines it is the advocates of scope and relevance who are the first to accept integration. Scepticism towards integration will be more prevalent among those who are doing more specialized work in theory or research. Perhaps the main problem, then, is not the integration of disciplines, but the development of workable combinations between broader more general approaches and the often more technical work of specialists, in both sociology *and* economics.

GPSR Compliance

The European Union's (EU) General Product Safety Regulation (GPSR) is a set of rules that requires consumer products to be safe and our obligations to ensure this.

If you have any concerns about our products, you can contact us on ProductSafety@springernature.com

In case Publisher is established outside the EU, the EU authorized representative is:

Springer Nature Customer Service Center GmbH
Europaplatz 3
69115 Heidelberg, Germany

Batch number: 10830937

Printed by Printforce, the Netherlands